4/7/13

My Memoirs

To Debby and Bruce,
Allison and Caroline,
your friendship mean
a lot to me and I
wish you all the
best.

Ameal Moore

My Memoirs

Climbing Up The Downstair Escalator

Ameal Moore

authorHOUSE®

AuthorHouse™
1663 Liberty Drive
Bloomington, IN 47403
www.authorhouse.com
Phone: 1-800-839-8640

Published by AuthorHouse   01/16/2013

ISBN: 978-1-4772-7096-7 (sc)
ISBN: 978-1-4772-7095-0 (hc)
ISBN: 978-1-4772-7221-3 (e)

Library of Congress Control Number: 2012917300

Contents

Foreword

At the urging of my wife, Henrietta, and my youngest sister Vera Mae Bullock, I decided to write my memoirs. I was hesitant for a long while but then thought it was a good idea, especially for my grandchildren, who range in age from seven to nineteen.

When I had completed the draft, I asked my good friend Sally Beaty if she would read it and make needed corrections. She did, and her input and suggestions were invaluable.

Sally is the wife of my dear friend Charles (Chuck) Beaty, PhD. When I first met Chuck, he was the principal at North High School. I served on the Site Council at his school and really got to know him. We got to know and respect each other well enough to disagree and still remain friends. Our friendship has grown over the years to the point that I consider him and Sally a part of the family—a friend close by is better than a brother far away.

Finally, I would like to thank everyone that supplied me with information, kindled my remembrance, and inspired and encouraged me. Thank you for seeing in me attributes I did not know I had.

My Memoirs:
Climbing Up the Down Escalator

As I sit here in my home office looking at the placards, awards, and proclamations I have received, I think how blessed I have been considering where I came from—a turpentine/logging camp in southern Mississippi where segregation was the rule. The only rights Black people (Negroes, Colored folk) had were what the White man allowed them to have. It was a system designed to foster the feeling of inferiority among people of color. I don't remember ever having a new school book—from the time I started public school until I graduated high school, the books were all hand-me-downs from the White schools. But I guess a book is a book is a book regardless of how well used. In fact, *use* can be a measure of its value.

Events in my life prepared me for the achievements I have accomplished: my eight years in the US Air Force in the security service with its variety of assignments; the people I met who encouraged me; going to college at night while working full time; and the murder of my brother Oneal, one of two Black deputy sheriffs, the first in Louisiana. These things were fertile ground for motivation and achievement. These experiences made me who I am.

I was born in Camp Rowling, a logging town in southern Mississippi. A logging camp moved about from place to place following the timber. My dad, Stephen Moore, supervised the making of crossties for the railroad for Mr. Lewis.

My dad bought a four-room bungalow house in 1938, and we became permanent residents on a ten-acre plot of land in White Sand, Mississippi, a rural area about five miles west of Poplarville, Mississippi. I was three or four years old when we moved to White Sand, so I don't remember much about the move. However, in the shadows of my mind, I recall sitting alongside the road for a while, probably due to a problem with the vehicle or wagon that transported us to our new home. We must have broken down somehow.

As far as I am aware, Mom, Dad, and seven children made the move: five boys and two girls, ranging in age from nineteen down to two. We moved into an area where there were about eight families within a mile of each other. Our nearest neighbor was down the lane about three hundred feet: Frank and Viola Silas and family. Up from us about the same distance was the family of John and Desline Travis, who moved from Camp Rowling around the time we did. A lane was a road between houses or fields on opposite sides, wide enough for a wagon or car to pass in either direction.

I had a happy childhood. I didn't know we were poor until years later. We always had food to eat and clothes to wear—maybe not store-bought but sufficient for our needs. When you are all in the same boat with everyone else, how do you know you are poor? The main thing is being happy and content in your situation.

When I was old enough, six or seven, Mom would send me down the lane, about a quarter mile, to the home of Amos and Ida Henry to get milk. One day when I made the trip, Miss Ida—we always called adults by their first name, honoring them with friendship and respect—asked me if I would like to have a puppy. I quickly said, "Yessum," and she gave me a gray looking puppy, which I took home along with a quart of milk.

As I walked with my puppy under one arm and a quart of milk under the other, my puppy licked my face, and I really fell in love with him before I made it home.

When Mom saw the puppy, I think she wanted me to take him back to Miss Ida, but she realized how much I wanted him, and she let me keep him. He was full of fleas, so Mom came up with a plan to rid him of them. While she was washing and boiling clothes in lye soap, she had me hold the puppy close to the fire around the boiling pot. True or not, we believe the fleas hopped off the puppy into the fire—all things are possible if you believe.

I named my puppy Sport. My brother Oneal, who was three years older than I was, would take Sport rabbit hunting with us. But instead of chasing rabbits, Sport would chase and bark at dry land turtles.

One day, a friend of mine named H. K. went swimming with me in a nearby creek. He had a non-identical twin named B. J. H. K. who was light-skinned and tall; B. J. was dark-skinned and hairy. In fact, his nickname was Fuzzy. While H. K. and I were swimming, Sport jumped in with us. When he came out, Sport was no longer gray—he was white. He had just been dirty.

I can remember when I first started school. I was six years old, and, of course, the school was segregated and held in the nearby Baptist church. I went to school there for a year or two and then the school moved to the Methodist Church for a year or so.

When the school was moved to the Methodist Church, there was a creek that ran nearby. In fact, we had to cross a bridge to get to the school. At recess, we worked to build a way to cross over the creek using tree limbs, dead wood, and whatever else was available—all without our teacher's knowledge. After several days' work, it was ready! The leader of the project, a boy named Leroy Nichols, asked who wanted to be the first to cross to the other side. I volunteered and fell into the creek.

About the same time, the bell rang and we had to return to class. The teacher, Mrs. Lester Bell Monday, saw that I was "ringing wet" and made me put on her daughter's dress. She always brought an extra dress to school for Shirley Ann, her daughter. From that day until the end of the semester, the kids never stopped teasing me.

The next year, the school moved into a newly built, large one-room school. I went there for one year before transferring to Pearl River County Training School in Poplarville. In May 1954, I graduated from high school in Poplarville.

While I was in high school, I drove the school bus that transported the students from White Sand to Poplarville. J. C. Monday was the owner of the bus. Mr. Monday lived across the creek about two miles east of where I lived. However, since I was the driver, I kept the bus at our family house.

I was a smart student and the principal, James Roy Todd, and his wife, Maggie Donna Todd, really motivated me to excel in my studies. When you are told you are a good student, it feeds your self-esteem. This made me study hard because I wanted to please them and continue to receive their praise and approval.

Several weeks after beginning at Pearl River County Training School, I remember defending myself after one of the teachers accused us "country bumpkins" of not being very bright. My response was that we were just as smart and capable of learning as anyone else. I said, "Just because we are from the country does not mean we are stupid and incapable of learning." I think my defense of our "country bumpkins" impressed Principal Todd and his wife Maggie, and they always had great respect for me after that.

A tragic accident involving the school bus took place one day on the way home from school. We were on a narrow road—a lane in each direction—when a stump truck driven by Jimmy Peters attempted to pass me. His view was obstructed by a curve in the road, and a car coming in the opposite direction swerved in front of me to avoid a head-on collision with the stump truck. I was traveling too fast to stop in time and crashed into the rear door of the car, fatally injuring the male passenger in the rear seat. The passenger died at the scene. I sustained an injury to my left knee which disabled me for about two weeks. No one else on the school bus was injured, thank God.

In high school, I was carried away by a big-eyed girl named Henrietta Silas. There were several girls that liked me and competed for my attention, but I really liked Henrietta who I later married. We have now been together for over fifty-four years at the time of this writing. I paid two dollars for the marriage license, and we were married by a justice of the peace, and his wife acted as the witness. My two-dollar investment in Henrietta was the best I ever made. She has been a faithful and loving wife.

Henrietta and I both enjoyed movies. When we began dating I cannot remember a weekend that we did not go to the movies—sometimes we even went during the week. Although we were only allowed to sit in the balcony, we nevertheless enjoyed attending. I must admit, though, that it made me angry to be told where we could or could not sit when we paid the same admission price as White moviegoers.

Another thing we enjoyed doing after the movies was eating chili dogs at a fast-food establishment in Bogalusa,

Louisiana. Even now when we go back to Mississippi to visit our relatives, we go back to the same fast-food restaurant and have chili dogs and strawberry malts. It brings back some very pleasant memories of intimacy, romance, and youth.

I graduated from high school in May 1954. I was the class president and valedictorian. The graduating class, however, only consisted of four students: two girls and two boys. The class motto was: "Preparing Today for Service Tomorrow." The school song was: In the year of 1919 our school was founded/With the stately yellow pines growing all around it/ This is where the boys and girls show their loyal spirits/What they do and what they say let the whole world hear it/School mates, school mates we'll be true/We'll be loyal ever/Pearl River County Training School/We'll forget, no, never.

That summer I worked with my brother-in-law, Clark Jordan, hauling stumps to a processing plant in Picayune, Mississippi. I believe ingredients for paint and turpentine were made from the stumps. For three years during high school, I hauled stumps during summer breaks.

Stumps were the tree stubs left in the ground after the trees had been cut down for lumber. The stumps were pushed out of the ground with a bulldozer, blown up with dynamite, trimmed with an axe, loaded on a truck, and hauled to the plant in Picayune, Mississippi for processing. My dad owned a truck, and I worked with my brother Oneal or Clark each summer.

Later in the summer of 1954, I took a job laying waterline pipe to a new garment factory in Poplarville, The Movie Star. I say "took" because I told the White foreman I needed a job, and, without waiting for his answer I joined in and began digging and laying pipe with everyone else. It worked; I got paid.

Colorful People from My Community

Mose Nichols was Leroy's father. I mentioned Leroy earlier—he was the leader in building our dam across the creek during recess. Mose Nichols was a colorful individual. He enjoyed showing off to friends and acquaintances how he had trained Leroy. He had developed a unique way of whistling. Whenever Leroy heard that whistle, no matter what he was doing or where he was, he came running to his dad like a puppy. I thought he treated Leroy like an animal instead of a human being, which displeased me. But Mr. Nichols took pride in showing off this trick.

Mose's wife Sophie loved to fish and was very good at it. She could catch fish when those with her never even got a bite. She told me once about a memorable fish she had caught. She said, "I caught a fish as wide as my hand, Leroy's hand, and Pearl Lee's (Leroy's older sister) hand put together." Now folks, that had to be a pretty big fish! I must have been in the seventh or eight grade when Mrs. Nichols told this story. I believe it was immediately following a very productive day of fishing.

Another individual in the community, Ben Harry, slept by the fireplace in his home. At least, I thought he did, because every time I went by, I found him lying by the fireplace. Uncle Ben, as we called him, was a con artist. I can remember him saying to me, "Ameal, you are a fine boy. I was telling my sons the other day what a fine boy you are. Now why don't you give old Unc' a dollar or two so I can buy something nice for myself?" Then he would burst out laughing. I enjoyed listening to the songs Uncle Ben spontaneously made up. Here are the words to one: I'm a big-time millionaire/I have money to loan, money to spend/I have enough money to give the poor and my kin/I'm a big-time millionaire.

And then there was a gentleman by the name of Simon Hart—everyone called him Pete. He had a unique way of speaking that made him appear to be in control even when he was dealing with his superiors—Black or White. For example, he told the White owner of the service station where he purchased gas for his stump truck and where he had it serviced, "I'm going to pay you your money, the money I owe you, but I am not going to pay it right now. I have other things I have to do first." Pete rendered the owner speechless.

The little town near where we lived was called Poplarville. It had a population of perhaps a thousand people at the most, counting those from surrounding country farms. Pete would say, "I'm going to town." And someone might say, "Can I go with you?" Pete's response would be, "I'm going to Hattiesburg; Poplarville is not a town but a village." When he would tell his wife, Guider he was going to town—Hattiesburg—she might ask him if he had his knife. Pete would chuckle and say, "I'm not going anywhere until you give me some sugar."

Pete was a neat dresser, but I don't believe he'd ever been to see a dentist except to have the occasional tooth pulled. Fun-loving guys in the community would tell this tale and attribute the statement to Pete, "You see my teeth. I have never had anything done to them." Pete got no argument from the audience on that one. Better hygiene would have greatly improved the appearance of his teeth.

I like proud men (not arrogant men); they inspire me. Someone has said, "If you do what you said you were going to do, it ain't bragging."

My brother Curtis, whose nickname was Sugar Pie, was a colorful individual. He and his wife Myrtle Lou Silas got married at a very young age—they were both in their teens. Interestingly, I ended up marrying Myrtle's sister, Henrietta Silas.

Sugar Pie was a very colorful man. He was a fun-loving guy that had a slight speech impediment that helped to accentuate his humor. He would tell you a story and screw up the punch line, but it would still turn out to be funny, because he would put his own spin on it, and his speech impediment gave it flavor.

Growing up, I enjoyed spending time at Sugar Pie and Myrtle's home. They built a recreational room about fifty feet from their house and equipped it with a stove, a counter, and a record player—a Wurlitzer. On Sundays, before and after church services, us teenagers would congregate in their room to eat, dance, and have a great time. I would guess that as many as ten to fifteen of us at a time would gather there. It was not until many years later that I realized just how small this room was and marveled that it had held so many of us. Sugar Pie and Myrtle relocated the room closer to their house and used it as a shed. To this day, as I write down this information, I marvel at how ten to fifteen teenagers could have danced and had such fun in such a small space.

Enlisted in US Air Force

After giving some serious thought as to what I was going to do the rest of my life, I decided to go into the air force. I had a working scholarship to attend Alcorn A&M College, working in the dairy, but I wanted to help provide for Mom and Dad. After obtaining my parents' approval, I went to the air force recruiter's office in Poplarville, and the next day I was on my way by Greyhound bus to Camp Shelby in Hattiesburg, Mississippi.

I joined a lot of other recruits and volunteers at Camp Shelby, where we were given physical examinations. Later that evening, they bussed us to the airport. They flew us to Lackland Air Force Base (AFB) in San Antonio, Texas. This was my first time on an airplane, and I can't describe how excited I felt.

When we landed at Lackland AFB, we boarded buses and went first to the mess hall and had a midnight meal before we were bussed to our barracks.

Early the next morning, Drill Instructor Mensendick yelled us out of bed, and into an activity-filled-day. There was breakfast, supplies, uniforms, haircuts, etc. Speaking of haircuts, I remember a young recruit with a beautiful head of hair—an Italian—who broke down crying after his hair cut. The barber asked him how he'd like his hair trimmed. He described, in great detail, how he wanted it cut. The barber smiled and went straight down the middle of his hair and ended up giving him a very close cut, just like the rest of us. That day I think we started to realize that we were no longer our own; we belonged to Uncle Sam, and if he said "jump" we said "how high."

The drill instructor selected me to be the second squad leader. With shoulders straight and head high, I was a proud squad leader. From basic training and throughout my eight years of military service, I enjoyed participating in and watching parades.

After leaving—completing—basic training at Lackland AFB, my next assignment was at an air base in Cheyenne, Wyoming, where I studied telecommunications. Telecommunication —among other things—consisted of learning to type at no less than forty words per minute. I still remember one of the typing drills: JUJ space, JUJ space, etc. We also had to learn to read teletype tape. Each character on the tape was shaped differently and represented a letter of the alphabet. The tape was used to transmit classified information—scrambled—from sender to receiver.

I was stationed in Cheyenne for about four months—February-May, 1955. I remember going into the city of Cheyenne with some White friends and was refused service at a restaurant. This made me realize that racial prejudice was not just confined to the South, where I was raised, but was institutionally ingrained in America's culture.

It is said that Cheyenne has two seasons: winter and Frontier Days. Frontier Days is the premier event of the year in Cheyenne. As for winter, there was snow on the ground when we arrived at Cheyenne and snow on the ground when we left. I was very happy to leave Cheyenne for my next assignment at Scott Field, Illinois.

At Scott Field, I was trained in cryptography—the art of encoding and decoding of highly classified information. I successfully obtained top secret and cryptographic clearance. My barrack at Scott Field was adjacent to the flight line. Every night at the same time, about three oclock in the morning, a jet took off. During my first week there, it woke me up every night. After the first week, though, I no longer noticed it. In fact, one night the jet did not take off, and I woke up. My sleep cycle had become intertwined with the jet's takeoff schedule.

The nearest town to Scott Field is Bellville, Illinois. I remember catching the bus in Bellville to St. Louis, Missouri to watch the St. Louis Cardinals. It was extremely exciting for me because I had never seen a major league baseball game. Of course I was an avid baseball fan and listened to games on the radio, but I had never been to a major league game before.

The bus to the ball park traveled through the neighborhood of East St. Louis. Any discomfort I felt about coming from the country (compared with my urban colleagues) evaporated while riding through the slums of East St. Louis. I had never seen so much trash, graffiti, dilapidated houses, and broken-down automobiles in all my days growing up in the country. We were poor, but we took pride in our surroundings. We made our surroundings clean and comfortable.

Harry Carey was the announcer for the St. Louis Cardinals, and a very colorful announcer he was. If you were listening to him while watching the game, you would wonder if the two of you were watching the same game. Harry later became the voice of the Chicago Cubs, where he broadcast their games until he died. He was famous for leading the Cubs fans in "Take Me Out to The Ball Game" during the seventh-inning stretch. He was also noted for saying, "the Cubs win, the Cubs win," whenever the Cubs won, which was rare.

After completing my training at Scott Field, I was assigned overseas duty at Clark AFB in the Philippines. I had a week's furlough before shipping out, so I went home by train to Poplarville, Mississippi to visit family and my girlfriend, Henrietta. I had a great time, but I was excited about my next assignment in the Philippines.

Voyage to the Philippines

I shipped out in September, 1955 from Travis AFB in San Francisco, California on the Fred C. Ainsworth, a troop carrier that was making its last voyage.

As we boarded the ship, I could smell a faint odor of vomit. Little did I know at the time that I would soon contribute to that odor. We ran into a storm the third day out at sea. We were in the mess hall watching a movie when the storm hit. In a short, many of us became seasick left the mess hall in search of the latrine. By the time I got there, the latrine was full of vomiting airmen. I hurried to my quarters, climbed into my rack (bunk), and breathed through my mouth, which gave me some relief.

I felt better the next morning, so I decided to go to the mess hall for breakfast; this proved to be a bad decision. The ship was tossing and turning, and my stomach was doing the same. I decided to go up on deck, thinking the fresh air would give me some relief. It was not so. Guys were hanging over the rail of the ship vomiting, and I joined in. A petty officer, a seasoned veteran of the seas, told me I needed to eat something or I would end up with dry heaves. He suggested I go to the ship's store and buy some soda crackers. I did and was able to weather the storm. In any event, by evening I had acquired my sea legs, and my stomach had settled down.

We were at sea twenty-one days. We were informed by the ship's crew that we lost a day transferring a very sick person to a ship heading to the United States. Also, we docked at Kwajalein Island and at Guam. We docked at Subic Bay, Philippines twenty-one days after leaving San Francisco. Military buses awaited our arrival and dispatched us to Clark AFB, on the Island of Luzon.

The Philippines is made up of several islands, the island of Luzon being the largest. Because of the many islands comprising the Philippines, the inhabitants speak many different dialects. The official language on Luzon is Tagalog.

Clark AFB, Philippines

We settled into our barracks and the next day began the work we had been trained to do—send and receive highly classified information.

The building that we—security service personnel—worked in also housed the intercept operators. Intercept operators deciphered the Morse code they received concerning the movement of aircraft and other information.

We worked hard, but we also had fun off duty. We had lots of fun in the barracks. I had never heard so many lies in all my life. Everyone participated, including me. We also spent some of our free time in the city of Angeles, which was right outside the base.

I remember listening to the final game of the 1955 World Series between the New York Yankees and the Brooklyn Dodgers while lying in my bunk in the wee hours of the morning. The Dodgers won the final and seventh game of the series 2-0. It was the only series the Dodgers won in Brooklyn. I was elated because I was a dyed-in-the-wool Dodgers fan because of Jackie Robinson, who had broken baseball's color line.

In the city of Angeles, my buddies patronized the Loma Linda Bar & Grill. It was owned by a Black man—we called him Pops—from Philadelphia, Pennsylvania who was married to a Filipino woman. Pops and his wife employed very attractive waitresses, so they had no shortage of customers. I was not a drinker, so I was the one to make sure that Eddie Barbee, James Speight, and Eddie Battle returned safely to the base. They would often get drunk. Once, someone got drunk—I believe it might have been Speight who was a well developed airman—and hit a carriage pony—a small horse—in the nose and knocking him to the ground. Poor horse; he wasn't doing anything.

It was an adventure to ride a bus to the city of Manila. Passengers would be hanging out the windows, and the driver would stop anywhere along the highway when passengers needed to relieve themselves. In any event, we enjoyed visiting Manila.

Baguio, a mountain resort, was another place I thoroughly enjoyed. It is located in the mountains of Cordillera. It is about four and half hours by bus from Clark AFB. We spent a very relaxing weekend there, enjoying the scenery, before returning to work.

After I completed my eighteen-month tour of duty at Clark AFB, my next assignment was in the USA. On my way back to the states, I spent the night at Hickam AFB in Hawaii. Before reporting to my next assignment at Lockport AFS, New York, I married my high school sweetheart, Henrietta.

Lockport Airport Station is in upstate New York, about thirty miles east of Buffalo, New York and Niagara Falls. I don't remember much about Buffalo, but I recall visiting Niagara Falls on several occasions. The Falls are a sight to behold, and I delighted in each visit. There's a beautiful, floral garden near the Canadian Falls, which I visited several times

I was stationed at Lockport for approximately four months before being reassigned to the National Security Agency (NSA) at Fort Meade, Maryland. After spending the night at a hotel in Rochester, New York, we drove the down to Fort Meade, Maryland. It was autumn, and the trees were beautiful with brown and gold leaves. It was a very pleasant drive.

When we arrived at Fort Meade, the NSA had not yet officially opened. In any event, we were bussed to our assignment at Arlington Hall in Virginia. The route to Arlington Hall took us to the Pentagon, where we dropped off officers and enlisted men who worked there. The bus consisted of individuals who were stationed at Ft. Meade from bases throughout the USA.(Army, Navy, Airforce and Marines). The Pentagon was particularly congested at the beginning and end of the work day, and I was quite fascinated with the volume of automobile traffic and people.

We worked at Arlington Hall for about a month, sending and receiving highly classified information, before moving into the National Security Agency at Fort Meade. If you recall, I got married to my high school sweetheart upon my arrival from the Philippines. In anticipation of Henrietta's joining me on my new assignment, I had rented an upstairs apartment in the home of a Washington, DC family and bought a used car, a Mercury, in order to commute to the NSA.

I really enjoyed working at the NSA and took pride in the work we were doing. It made me feel important that I was doing some very special work for my country. I guess my enthusiasm for my work caught the attention of a Black officer who suggested I apply for officer candidate school. I followed his advice and visited personnel to find out how to proceed. During this process, I discovered the name on my birth certificate, Ellian, was different from the name used on all other records, which was Ameal. The person I spoke to in personnel suggested I get a notarized letter from my parents indicating Ellian and Ameal were the same person. But before I could obtain this information, I was reassigned to Thule AFB, Greenland.

Before my assignment to Thule, I had reenlisted for another four years traded in my Mercury for a 1958 Ford. That December, Henrietta and I drove home to spend the Christmas holidays with our parents.

Shortly after we arrived in Mississippi, Henrietta's father, Henry Silas, had a stroke. He was in Deridder, Louisiana, which was a good distance away from White Sand, Mississippi. Anyway, Henrietta's mother Orta Bell, her son Wiley Silas, Henrietta, and I drove to Deridder. Henry Silas was alive in the hospital when we arrived but died the next day. By the way, Henrietta was pregnant with our first son, Jeffery, when we came home from Washington, DC. She did not go to the hospital where her Dad was but stayed at his house in Deridder.

Henry Silas was a proud and benevolent person. He could not read or write, but he was a businessman who owned a stump truck and a bulldozer. When stumps became scarce in Mississippi, he and his family relocated to Deridder, Louisiana. Of course, they kept their home in White Sand, Mississippi. Mr. Silas owned quite a bit of land. In fact, he donated the land and built a school in the White Sand community. Additionally, he and his wife Orta Bell always provided food and lodging for the less fortunate kids in the area.

Following the funeral services, Henrietta and I returned to Washington, DC.

During the two years I lived in Washington, DC (1957-1959), three civilian employees carpooled to work with me: Jeanette Hughes, Helen Mosley, and Josephine Norwood. We became close friends and really enjoyed each other's company. We would resolve the problems of the world on our trips back and forth to work.

My first son, Jeffery Ameal, was born at Walter Reed Army Hospital. I was a nervous wreck the night Henrietta came down with labor pains, and I rushed her to the hospital. I was prepared to wait in the waiting room until Henrietta gave birth, but the nurse sent me home and told me they would call when the baby arrived. It was 1959, and spouses were not allowed in the delivery room with their wives. In the early morning hours, I received a call from Walter Reed Hospital that Henrietta had given birth.

I was a proud father when I picked up my wife and son from the hospital and held my son in my arms for the first time. Additionally, when we arrived back at our upstairs apartment in the home of E. J. and Lena Witherspoon, they were just as excited. You would think they were grandparents instead of landlords. In fact, they considered themselves Jeffery's grandparents, which were a great comfort to Henrietta and me.

Before I move on to my next assignment at Thule, let me tell you about an event that touched Henrietta's and my heart. At that time, the air force paid its employees every two weeks. Well, for some reason I no longer remember, we ran out of money and food about two or three days before payday. There Henrietta and I sat in our small apartment trying to determine how we were going to resolve our situation. While we were pondering our options—try to get food on credit or pawn something—there was a knock on the door. It was Audrey Snyder; she and her husband Jack rented the upstairs apartment across from us. She had just returned from some function and had brought home enough food to feed a family for several days. Audrey shared that food with us, and it lasted until payday. The Lord works in mysterious ways. We never forgot Audrey's kindness and gave our heartfelt thanks to God for sending Audrey to us.

Thule, Greenland

After driving Henrietta and Jeffery to Mississippi to stay with her mother while I was away, I made my way to McGuire AFB in New Jersey and boarded a plane to Thule, Greenland.

We spent the night at Goose Bay, Labrador. There I witnessed the magnificent display of the northern lights—aurora borealis. Wow! It was awe-inspiring! The next morning we boarded the plane on the last leg to Greenland. By the way, Greenland is not green; it's ice. The Danish gave it the name Greenland in order to convince people to move there. The basic population is Eskimo. In contrast, Iceland has some greenery. Thule has none and lies within the Arctic Circle. The year is divided: six months of daylight and six months of darkness.

When we arrived at the airbase in Greenland, it was covered in fog, and there was too much fog to land. The pilot circled the area for quite some time, waiting for a break in the weather. When a break in the fog did not occur, the pilot decided to fly to Sondrestrom AFB, Greenland. When we landed there, the pilot informed us that we had only about half hour of fuel left in the plane.

We spent the night at Sondrestrom, refueled the plane, and flew back to Thule the next morning. This time we were able to land; the fog had cleared.

The first thing we did after landing was check out arctic gear at the base's supply station. One thing I can say about arctic gear is that it's well designed: the parka, the hood, the boots, and the gloves will keep you warm in the frigid weather of the arctic.

A few weeks after settling in at Thule, we—security service personnel—our unit was deactivated. Everyone was reassigned to security bases away from Thule except for me and another airman whose name I don't recall. He and I were transferred to the Strategic Air Command (SAC) and remained at Thule. This felt like a demotion to me, and I knew then that I would not reenlist again.

There were only a few recreational activities at Thule, and I chose bowling and the service club. A service is a place where recreational activies are available and refreshments. I recall once while bowling solo, a Black officer—a pilot—asked to join me. When I noticed that he was an officer I said, "I am just a staff sergeant and you want to bowl with me?" He responded, "Mocks nix(who cares); let's bowl." I think I let him win the game.

The barracks at Thule was the antithesis of a refrigerator—it kept the hot air in and the cold air out. They had a very efficient heating system except when they lost electricity.

High winds, known as phases, occur at Thule and create blinding snow storms. The snow at Thule has very little moisture; you can't make a snowman out of it. Therefore, when phases occur, they whip the loose snow into a blinding storm. I recall a phase that knocked out the power in our barrack. We all assembled in the boiler room to keep warm until power could be restored. It was quite a while before it was restored, and I believe all of us became fearful but said nothing. Like good airmen, we weathered the storm.

One of our favorite pastimes in the barracks was watching cartoons: Bugs Bunny, Foghorn Leghorn, the Road Runner, Yosemite Sam, etc. We would be in our rooms writing letters, playing cards, or sleeping, but when we heard the cartoon music, we rushed to the dayroom.

The year I spent at Thule was the longest year of my life. What sustained me most were the letters I wrote to Henrietta and the letters I received from her. It was a comfort to me to know that she was okay and that our son Jeff was growing like a weed.

Looking back, I am grateful for the experience of serving at Thule, but I never wanted to do it again.

Finally, it was time to pack my bags and head home to see my wife and son before going to my next assignment at March AFB in California. It was great to reunite with my wife, my son, and other family members, and they made me feel very special and appreciated. I'm not sure why, but I didn't overthink it. I accepted their love and appreciation and moved on.

One disturbing bit of information Henrietta shared with me made me angry. The local police department in Poplarville had threatened to arrest her if she did not get Mississippi license plates for our 1958 Ford, even though I was away serving my country in Greenland. To avoid the situation, she took the car and left it with my brother Oneal and his family in Varnado, Louisiana.

After spending a couple of weeks with my relatives, Henrietta, Jeff, and I hit traveled to Riverside, California. Along the way, lodging was scarce to nonexistent for Black folk. For the most part, we slept in the car and freshened up at service stations where we purchased gasoline. Even this was not without conflict. I remember a service station manager scolding my wife for washing and cleaning up Jeffery in the station's restroom. It really made me angry, but there wasn't anything I could do about it. It was not until we reached El Paso, Texas that we were able to obtain lodging. Even then, we were relegated to the hotel basement and its lumpy mattress. It was not until we arrived in Phoenix, Arizona that we were able to obtain lodging and accommodations in a newly constructed motel. We felt welcome, had a nice meal, and got a good night's sleep.

Arriving in Riverside, California in the late afternoon, we spent the night at the Riverside Hotel on Eighth Street, now University Avenue. After a restful night's sleep, we focused on finding an apartment. We were fortunate to rent an apartment on the corner of Tenth Street and Park Avenue. It was a recently constructed three-story apartment complex. We rented a one-bedroom apartment and bought furniture the next day.

I was assigned to the thirty-third communication squadron, which was stationed on a hill about three to five miles from

March AFB. There I spent the remainder of my enlistment, two and half years, working shifts sending and receiving messages. The classification of these messages was nowhere near the level of classification I had become accustomed to in the security service, so I no longer felt excited by my work.

The scenery really sold Henrietta and me on Riverside and the surrounding area. There were palm trees, orange groves and their fragrance, and the beautiful snow-capped mountains that paint such a lovely picture in winter. I am still in awe of the beautiful scenery. Another part of Riverside that fascinated me was Victoria Avenue: the huge eucalyptus trees along the avenue and the orange groves were a site to behold. On many Sunday afternoons, I would drive down Victoria Avenue to meditate and relax.

Our second son—Derwin Stephen—was born April 29, 1961, about nine months—give or take—after I returned home from Thule. A close friend of ours, George Suel, called him a "Thule baby." George had served at Thule also, but at a different time, and lived in the eastside community of Riverside.

Doctor Watts, a medical doctor at March AFB, informed Henrietta and me that Derwin (who we called Steve) had an enlarged heart and arranged for us to see a doctor in San Diego and another one at UCLA for a second opinion. If I remember correctly, both doctors said there was nothing to worry about. They told us that Steve would grow out of the problem. This was a big relief, as we had grown very concerned about the situation. Steve does have a big heart, both figuratively and literally.

Honorable Discharge

I was honorably discharged from the Air Force on November 30, 1962. I immediately began applying for work in the communication field. I applied to Norton AFB, Western Union, and the Foreign Service. I also took the Postal Service examination.

In the meantime, I worked with a friend and independent contractor, Harold Rainey, preparing vacant houses for sale. We plastered, painted, patched holes, and more. I did this until I began work as a letter carrier with the US Postal Service in May, 1963.

It is ironic that I was approved for the Foreign Service at the same time I began work at the Postal Service. If I had not already started working, I probably would have accepted the Foreign Service job. As the poet Robert Frost said, "two roads diverged in a yellow wood," and I took the one that eventually led to the fulfillment of a dream.

My first day as a letter carrier tested my resolve. It was a very warm day, and I was assigned a bicycle route. It was a gruesome day, and I was loaded down with lots of letters and advertisements. Additionally, a customer confronted me and cursed me with every expletive she could think of. It was the beginning of the month, and I didn't have her welfare check. She was livid! She said, "Every time we get a new mailman, he loses my check." With that abuse and the physical exhaustion of pedaling the bicycle all day, I didn't know if I really wanted to be a mail carrier.

At home that evening, I debated whether or not I would go to work the next day. I did and served thirty years with the US Postal Service.

My Brother Oneal

My brother Oneal and I were very close even though he was three years older. Oneal liked to build things. At an early age, he learned to build wagons, kites, bird houses, etc. We used the wagons to haul the firewood we gathered from open land. Once we loaded the wagon, Oneal would pull and I would push it home.

Oneal was very courageous. I never saw him back down from a challenge. He was also very fair-minded: he was very fair in his dealings and expected to receive the same treatment in return. It didn't matter if you were Black or White: Oneal expected you to be fair with him.

I remember Oneal getting into a dispute with his employer's son-in-law. He was about eighteen at the time. The son-in-law operated the bulldozer that pushed the stumps out of the ground. Oneal was in the process of climbing upon the bulldozer when Vick, the son-law operator, drove away. Of course, Oneal jumped from the bulldozer. This is just one example of Oneal's courage and aggressiveness.

In February 1965, I rode the Greyhound bus from Riverside to Poplarville, Mississippi to visit my parents and relatives.

While I was there, I spent some time with Oneal and his family in Varnado, Louisiana.

Oneal and Creed Rogers, both Black, had recently been appointed deputy sheriffs in Louisiana. They were the first Blacks to be appointed in Louisiana, at least as far as I'm aware. While I sat in the living room chatting with Oneal and his wife Mavella, I began kidding Oneal about his position of deputy sheriff. I said, "A deputy sheriff, huh? Show me your tin badge." Oneal got up and left the room. In a short while, he came back fully dressed in his uniform. He pointed to his badge and said, "This ain't a tin badge." I knew then that he was extremely proud of his appointment and didn't want to hear any nonsense.

That night, I tagged along with Oneal and Creed and experienced the potential danger they faced while patrolling their beat. On a moonless night in the piney woods of Louisiana, it is so dark you can only see a few feet in front of you. They could have easily been ambushed. They were, in fact, ambushed very close to Oneal's home, less than a mile, in June 1965, about four months after I returned home to Riverside. I didn't get to see Oneal before I left for California because he was away helping to build a house in Bogalusa, Louisiana, when I left.

I was in bed after a difficult delivery day at the post office when the phone rang; it was Myrtle Moore my sister-in-law notifying me that Oneal had been killed by so-called night riders (KKK), and his partner Creed Rogers seriously wounded.

Nothing has ever made me as angry as Oneal's death. However, I cannot say I was surprised. To this day, no one has been brought to justice for the murder of my brother Oneal, and the Sheriff's department never made any effort to finding the people involved and bringing them to trial. This proves to me that the White deputies in the Sheriff's department didn't support Oneal and Creed. They had only appointed Oneal and Creed to make a show of equality, but they gave them no support.

It was years before I was able to get rid of my anger and bitterness. I read all kinds of things—magazines, books, and stories—to try to make sense of my brother's murder. Gradually, it dawned on me that he had helped to open doors to African Americans. Change, I learned, does not come without sacrifice. I learned about many others who lost their lives during the civil rights movement, both Black and White. Many years after Oneal's death, Nelson Mandela's book, *Long Walk to Freedom,* put things in perspective for me and helped me overcome my last trace of bitterness. As you may know, Mandela was a prisoner in South Africa for twenty-seven years. He spent eighteen years on Robben Island and the remaining nine years at Pollsmoor and Victor Verster prisons.

I once read a statement attributed to Mandela. A reporter asked him if he was bitter after serving twenty-seven years as a prisoner. His response was, "I want to be free, and I can't be free if I am bitter." That statement made me realize that I was a prisoner of my own bitterness. It was eating away inside of me. I became the victim. To let go of that anger and bitterness freed me to move forward.

In 1989, the Southern Poverty Law Center in Montgomery, Alabama, invited Mavella—Oneal's widow—and our entire family to participate in the opening of a memorial in memory of individuals who had lost their lives during the civil rights movement in the South. My brother Oneal was included in the memorial. Mavella gave me permission to speak on behalf of the family. I took advantage of the opportunity and eulogized the life of my beloved brother. Below is a draft of the speech I gave followed by a letter to Morris Dees, Director of the Southern Poverty Law Center.

It is an honor and a privilege to be here this evening on this historic occasion. I am bursting with pride as I stand before you.

We are deeply indebted to those of you that have made this event possible. Your vision and hard work have assured a place in history for all the men and women who gave their lives during the struggle for freedom and equality in this great nation of ours.

When I was asked if I would like to speak on this occasion, I did not hesitate to seize the opportunity. I and the family of Oneal Moore were and are very proud of him and the memories he left us. I am therefore very proud and pleased to say a few words at an event were his name is being memorialized.

It is only fitting that a memorial be erected to honor the brave men and women who gave their lives in the struggle for freedom and equality. Some are better known than others because of the way their lives were snuffed out. But all were victims of racial prejudice. They dared to take a stand where cowards would not dare to tread. They challenged a system that denied them and their race their basic human rights.

Those who are memorialized here lived during a period of total segregation—separate schools, separate lunch counters, separate accommodations, separate drinking fountains, and seats in the back of the bus. The Klan and White supremacy groups were rampant and a Black man's life was not worth a plugged nickel. During this time, a Black man was fair game for a lynch mob or night riders.

They took the lives of these brave young men and women who are memorialized here today, but they could not put out the fire that these brave souls helped to kindle. There is no stopping a "dream whose time has come." The methods by which their lives were taken angered decent law abiding citizens of this nation—both Black and White. The conscience of this nation was aroused with righteous indignation. White men and women joined hands with their Black brothers and sisters, and the walls of segregation began to crumble and fall.

It is only fitting that the memorial be erected here in the city of Montgomery, in the state of Alabama, the heart of the Confederacy; the state where so many civil rights battles were fought. This is a state where the governor stood in the school house door. Marchers were hosed down, attacked by dogs, beaten, and thrown in jail. It was from the Birmingham jail where Dr. King—that great leader of the civil rights movement—penned his famous letter to the clergy of this nation. He answered their criticism of the movement. With simplicity and eloquence he told them why we cannot wait. The wait had been too long already. In essence: "Justice delayed is justice denied."

Without knowledge of our history, we are without roots. There is a need to know why you are what you are. In order to have a clear understanding of where we are trying to go, it is important to know where we came from; to know why we are traveling the road we are traveling and dreaming the dreams we are dreaming. I think the memorial will help us and generations yet unborn to realize the cost of freedom; to remember the evil and viciousness of racial prejudice; to remember the sacrifice of human lives in the struggle for freedom and justice. Thanks to this memorial, the memories that we family members carry in our hearts can be shared with a nation that needs to remember. When we look back at where we have been and how far we have come, we can say with uplifted voices, "Free at last! Free at last! Thank God Almighty, we are free at last!"

Morris Dees, Director   11-11-89
Southern Poverty Law Center

Dear Mr. Dees:

What an exhilarating experience! The Civil Rights Memorial is a fitting tribute to those who lost their lives during the struggle for freedom and equality.

I don't know the faith to which you belong, but I believe God inspired you and the Southern Poverty Law Center to build the memorial. It gives meaning to the lives of those who died during the struggle. All family members can now be assured that our loved ones whose lives were cut short did not die in vain. Thanks to the memorial, their names will live in history and will, I believe, inspire us and generations yet unborn to greater achievements.

Thank you, Mr. Dees, and may God shower his blessings upon you.

Sincerely,

Ameal Moore
Brother of Oneal Moore

After the program, I met with the son of George Wallace. He was a diminutive man about five feet six inches tall but gracious and apologetic about his father and the pain and heartache he caused Black people. In fact, George Wallace himself became the victim of an attempted assassination. For the most part, Black caretakers attended to him afterward.

This was my first visit to Montgomery, Alabama's capital. I was amazed at the close proximity of the state capitol building and Dexter Avenue Church, where Martin Luther King Jr. was the pastor during the Montgomery bus boycott. Governor Wallace stood at the capitol saying, "segregation forever," and Dr. King, who became the leader of the civil rights movement, saying, "These unjust laws must be done away with and segregation must end."

The monument in front of the Southern Poverty Law Center is very beautiful; it is a fitting tribute to many of the lesser known heroes of the movement. The memorial in front of the Southern Poverty Law Center, is made of marble with a marble top, and the names of the fallen heroes are carved around the edge of the marble circle. In the center is a fountain of water that spews up and spreads out very thinly over the entire marble top.

The men and women honored by the memorial are gone, but their memories and contributions to the civil rights movement live on here and in history. You can kill the dreamer, but the dream lives on. In fact, today we are living the dream. Dr. King shared the night before his assassination: "I have been to the mountaintop, I have looked over, and I have seen the promised land. I may not get there with you, but you will get to the promised land."(Dr. King).

Back to School

One educational asset where I grew up was Pearl River County Junior College, a two-year institution of learning. It had the reputation of being one of the best, if not the best, junior colleges in the state of Mississippi. Of course this was when facilities were segregated and Black students could not attend this institution. I went into the Air Force after graduating from high school in 1954, and when I returned from the Philippines in 1957, Black students still were not able to attend. It was not until 1967-68 that Black students were integrated there.

I tell you the above story because I think it ties in very well with a situation that took place on a Carnival Cruise many years later, in 2001, when I was a Riverside city councilman. This was the third cruise wife Henrietta and I and I had taken, and we enjoyed every one of them. On this cruise we met the President of Pearl River Junior College—Mr. Williams. We were dinner guests together during the entire cruise. In addition, we discovered we were both Rotarians. We thoroughly enjoyed each other's company and chatted extensively on many different subjects. When I revealed to him that I was a Rotarian and that I was from White Sand, a suburb of Poplarville, he invited me to be his guest at a Rotary meeting held at Pearl River Junior College. In the summer of 2003, when my wife Henrietta and I visited our relatives in Mississippi, I contacted Mr. Williams. He confirmed his invitation to me and gave me the details of the Rotary meeting.

It just so happens that my niece Delores Henry worked at the college in the cafeteria and was delighted when she became aware that I was to be the guest of President Williams; she made it clear to anyone who would listen, both before and at the meeting, that I was her uncle.

We had a great Rotary meeting. President Williams introduced me as his guest, and I received a warm welcome from the club members. At my table sat Martin Smith, an attorney and a former state legislator. Mr. Smith was our family attorney, and he had great respect for my Dad, Stephen who died in 1989. He shared his memories of Dad with the other guests at our table. I felt very welcome and left the meeting pleased with the experience. It was a different place from the college I knew growing up. People can change, but it is not always easy. *One constant in this world is change. You can accept it and learn to live with it, or you can reject it and be miserable.*

My academic education was put on hold during my eight years of military service. After I left the service, I knew that I needed to complete college in order to achieve my potential in terms of both my employment and quality of life. It was with apprehension that I enrolled at Riverside Community College (RCC) in the fall of 1964. I didn't know if I was prepared for college work, and I was afraid of failure. Additionally, working full time and going to school at night was a challenge in itself.

I started my classes at RCC determined to do my best. Fortunately, I did well on my assignments, and the positive feedback I received gave me confidence. Also, many of my teachers and instructors were very encouraging: Mr. McArthur, Ms. Day, and Ms. Hickok to name a few. In 1970, I graduated with honors from RCC with an associate's degree in business administration with a concentration in accounting. In the spring of 1971, I enrolled at California State University, Fullerton (CSUF).

At CSUF, I applied the same determination I had at RCC. I didn't graduate with honors, but I graduated in 1974 with a bachelor's degree in business administration with a concentration in accounting.

After graduating from CSUF, I took the MBA entry examination at the University of Southern California in Los Angeles (USC). I passed the examination and was accepted into the MBA program at Cal Poly Technical College in Pomona. However, I did not attend.

I was so burned out after ten years of working full time and going to school at night that I no longer had the energy or determination to continue. It was the good Lord that watched over me during my drive home at night from CSUF. I know I had fallen asleep on many occasions because I do not remember many parts of those drives.

A Still, Soft Voice

One night while saying my prayers, a soft voice spoke to me—soft, but very clear. It said, "I have a very important position for you." I thought the voice was referring to a postmaster position, as that is what I was aspiring to be at the time.

I had acquired my BA in business administration in 1974 with a concentration in accounting. Through persistence and hard work, I had become a carrier supervisor, the first Black supervisor in the Riverside Postal Service. I was promoted from letter carrier to supervisor in 1974. Ten years later, in 1984, I was applying to postmaster positions whenever I heard of vacancies in the area. In fact, I was an acting postmaster in Mentone, California, a small town northeast of Redlands, California, in 1983.

Although I opened doors for other Blacks to become supervisors in the Riverside Postal Service and in the Inland Empire, the role of Postmaster eluded me. However, I never forgot that voice that said to me, "I have a very important position for you."

One night in 1974 following my graduation from CSUF, I received a telephone call from Dr. Lulamae Clemons, a respected Black leader in the community. We knew each other because we were both members of Second Baptist Church. She asked if I would be interested in becoming the president of the Riverside chapter of the NAACP. I felt honored to be considered for the position, but at the same time I was scared and unsure of my ability to lead this historic and prestigious organization. I told her I needed to talk to my family before giving her an answer.

After hanging up the phone, I met with my family: my wife Henrietta, Jeffery (15), Steve (13), and Carl (10). They were unanimous. They all told me to go for it! When I contacted Dr. Clemons the next day, she said Reverend Campbell of Allen Chapel Methodist Church had agreed to serve as president, but the organization wanted me to serve as vice president. I agreed to take the vice president position. About a year later, Reverend Campbell relocated to a different city and I became president.

Under my leadership, the board set a goal to get qualified Blacks in decision-making positions in all areas of the city. For five years or so, I met regularly with the city manager, chief of police, and RUSD (Riverside Unified School District) superintendent. I even served on committees for the school district, one of which established the criteria for high school graduation.

Riverside NAACP and Head Start

When I was the Riverside NAACP president, we had a program called Head Start. It prepared young children for public school. It was a very effective program in that the children from Head Start did very well in public school. Gaye Caroline was in charge of this program, and I commend her for the outstanding job she did in preparing the kids for regular public school. Gaye's husband, Mr. Caroline, was a retired Riverside policeman, one of the first Blacks, if not the first, to serve as a city policeman.

When I first became president, Head Start was located at Park Avenue and Tenth Street. Later, the school moved into a building owned by the City of Riverside located at University and Kansas, the site which is now Bobby Bond Park/Cesar Chavez Center. The founders of Head Start realized that our children are our future, and if they are to reach their full potential in life, they must be well educated and prepared for leadership. As president of the local chapter of the NAACP, I was well aware of the needs in Riverside and began to address them during my term as president. There were no Black school principals; no Black members of city council; and very few, if any, Blacks serving on boards and commissions for the city. As president, I set out to address these needs and was able to achieve some success. During my term as president, the first Black principal was appointed (Booker Huling), more Black policemen were hired, and I was selected by Mayor Loveridge to serve on the Parking, Traffic, and Streets Commission as well as the Planning Commission. Devonne Armstrong, a Black realtor, preceded me on the Planning Commission.

By the way, while I was president, I was successful in getting Joe Madison to speak at one of our banquets in the late 1970s. I don't remember where I met Joe; I can only say I was immediately impressed by him. At the time he was our banquet speaker, Joe had relatives in Victorville, California, and I had the pleasure of meeting them. Joe Madison currently has a syndicated radio program in the Washington, DC area and makes frequent appearances as a guest on Cable TV (MSNBC).

Marge Grass

For many years, Marge Grass served as the liaison between Arlington Avenue Methodist Church and Second Baptist Church. Arlington Methodist was/is predominately White, and Second Baptist was/is predominately African American. Her work brought us closer together in our Christian faith. After all, we worship the same God and believe that his son Jesus Christ came to earth, died for our sins, was buried, rose on the third day, and sits at the right hand of the father in heaven.

A friend of mine, Chodsie Goins, a very active member of Second Baptist and the wife of L. C. Goins, was a good friend of Marge Grass and worked very closely with her. Marge Grass attended the services at Second Baptist on a regular basis and arranged the annual exchange of services at Arlington Methodist. Second Baptist Choir rehearsed for weeks leading up to these special days, and Pastor Thomas delivered the message. Even though I was a member of the choir, I thought my role was insignificant. Well, about a year after my election to the city council in January 1994, I received a call from Marge Grass requesting that I share some comments at her funeral service. She was terminally ill, and it was just a matter of time. I couldn't say no to such a request;

though while I felt honored, I also felt very uncomfortable. Anyway, after Marge died, I honored her request and spoke at her funeral. I do not remember what I said, but it was from the heart.

Sid Francis

S id Francis was an outgoing, proud individual. When I first met Sid, I was the president of the local chapter of the NAACP and had lunch with him and City Attorney Woodhead at the restaurant on the corner of University Avenue and Mesa Street. Evidently Sid wanted to introduce me to some of the important people he knew in the city. My initial contact with Sid Francis grew into frequent contact. Sid was in the construction/development trade. His office was located on Arlington Avenue near Brockton Street. He had a partner, an attorney, by the name of Trevor Hamilton, who lived in Victorville, California. He later became a judge there. Sid and his partner had acquired some property southeast of Corona, along I-15, for development. He took Henrietta and me out to see it. I think he wanted to establish himself as a serious businessman and a strong supporter of the NAACP. I soon learned that Sid was a good friend of Peggy and Eddie Streeter. Peggy had a catering business—Peggy's Party Shop—on the corner of Fourteenth Street and Park Avenue, which was very successful. In addition to being a successful entrepreneur, she was a strong supporter of the NAACP, giving her time and financial support. Peggy was also the founder/organizer of a social club called The Elites, which was well-respected in the community. It attracted women who wished to give back to the community and gave them the opportunity to elevate their social image. In a nutshell, Peggy Streeter was a respected leader in the community and my staunch supporter and advisor.

Getting back to Sid Francis—he was a persuasive, charismatic individual who led the group who brought heavyweight champion Muhammad Ali to Riverside's Stratton Center in Bordwell Park. Wow! What an exciting day that turned out to be. I remember being among the group when Ali first appeared on the scene. He was a young, handsome, cocky champion, and I felt honored to be in his presence.

Sid was the type of guy who would do anything for his friends. When Henrietta and I celebrated our twenty-fifth wedding anniversary in 1982, Sid had a truckload of flowers delivered to our home on Celeste Drive. Sid died in the late '80s, but his memory is still with us today. He was a proud man, a man who did not let the color of his skin prohibit him from competing and achieving. Rest in peace, Sid; you fought a good fight and set a positive example for other people of color.

In 1978, as president of the NAACP, I endorsed Ronald Loveridge for councilman of the First Ward. Ron won the election, and in the early '80s, I was appointed to the Parking, Traffic, and Street Commission. About eight years later, I was appointed to the Planning Commission, where I served until I was elected to the city council in January 1994 as a representative of the Second Ward. This was ten years after that clear, soft voice said, "I have a very important position for you," and twenty years after I decided I wanted to be a councilman (1974).

I became interested in serving on the city council after watching a hearing in the council chambers involving a Black officer at University of California Riverside (UCR). I do not recall the details of the hearing, but it made me aspire to be a city councilman. In fact, in 1978 we moved to Celeste Drive in the University area, which was located in the Second Ward. I thought I had the best chance of being elected there.

In 1992 (November), after serving thirty years with the US Postal Service, I retired. Early in 1993, I received word that Jack Clarke Sr. (the first Black councilman in Riverside) was not going to run for another term. Perfect! This is what I had been waiting for. So I filed my papers and became a candidate for the council seat in the Second Ward. I attended every council meeting so that I was thoroughly familiar with the issues. I was there so regularly that I believe I could have served in the absence of a regular council member without missing a beat.

The election was held in November of 1993. After filing my papers to become a candidate, I realized I needed a campaign manager. Someone put me in touch with a gentleman in the school system who was interested in politics and had an election strategy. He met with me in my home on Celeste Drive and outlined a plan of action. However, before we could get started on the plan, he retired and moved to Northern California.

At first I was very despondent. Even before I could really get started, I lost my campaign manager, and the so-called Black leaders in the ward were upset because I did not consult them. One in particular—Charles Carter—said I was not "strong enough" to be a councilman. He said, "I would vote for your wife, Henrietta, before I would vote for you." That is quite a tribute to my wife. She would have been a very strong council person.

Never let someone else define who you are. Determine for yourself who you are, and pursue your goal in life. Stay focused. That's when I learned, "Know thou self and to thine own self be true."

Anyway, I set about looking for a new campaign manager. First I asked myself what characteristics I wanted in a manager. They were: loyalty, trustworthiness, and competency. Voila! My longtime friend and one-time next-door neighbor, Dorothy Bailey fit the bill. Dorothy (Dottie) and I set about putting our plan into action with the boldness of two people who had never been involved in a political campaign. Below is the kickoff speech I delivered at Park Avenue Baptist Church.

With supreme authority, we know that it is more blessed to give than to receive. I must say then, that you are going to be blessed immeasurably for giving your time, your money, and your support here tonight. I am grateful beyond words to be the recipient of your generosity. We have lots of concerns in this city, but they are no different from any throughout the nation: unemployment, crime, gangs, drugs, and homelessness. You would think that we are regressing instead of progressing. But I am an optimist. I don't believe that any of our problems are so great that we can't collectively solve them. That's why I'm a candidate for all the people, not any particular ethnic group. The solution to our problems will come when families, our schools, churches, businesses, and government work together. As individuals, we need to shoulder our responsibilities and serve as positive role models to our children. Were Dr. King alive today, he would probably say to us, "Let's hue out of the mountain of despair a stone of hope." I want to be a stone of hope.

My name is Ameal: not lunch, not dinner, but Ameal. When I was born my Mom looked at me and said, "Mercy, he looks hungry." So she fed me and named me Ameal.

It is an honor and a privilege for me to kick off my campaign on the eve of Dr. Martin Luther King's sixty-third birthday. I can't think of a more appropriate way to celebrate his birthday. It was he that made it possible for me and other people of color to vote, run for elective office, and to actively participate in the political process. Indeed, he made participation possible in almost every area of this great nation, the only qualification be one's ability to do the job.

What are my qualifications? I have been actively involved in the city of Riverside since 1974. I served five years as president of the local chapter of the NAACP. As president, I guided and developed the local chapter from a floundering organization to an effective, dynamic force in this community. In the process, I gained the support and respect of the leaders of the city. Under my leadership, we secured a home for Head Start. I met monthly with the superintendant of RUSD, the city manager, and the chief of police. I served on the RUSD task force to determine test scores for graduating high school students. I also served on RUSD's strategic planning committee as well as the Greenbelt Study Committee for the City of Riverside.

I served on Riverside's Parking, Traffic, and Street Commission for seven years—three of those years as its chairman. I am currently serving my eighth and final year on the City Planning Commission. In 1990-1991, I served as its chairman. I served as chairman of the Greater Riverside Area Urban League from 1988 until its National Affiliation was obtained in 1990.

I have served as the chairman of the board of trustees at Second Baptist Church and am currently a board member.

For me, Dr. Martin Luther King was a Moses to his people. He set out to lead his people to the Promised Land in America, the milk and honey that was already being enjoyed by others. He told Governor Wallace of Alabama, "let my people go." He told Governor Faubus of Arkansas, "Let my people go." He told Bull Connors and Lester Maddox, "Let my people go." He told the White Citizens Council, "Let my people go." Indeed, he told the leaders of the nation, "Let my people go."

Dr. King's memory has a humbling and yet an inspiring effect upon me. You see, I was born in the segregated South; received a segregated education through high school; ate in segregated restaurants; drank from separate water fountains labeled "Colored"; rode the back of the bus; and slept in my car when traveling because public accommodations were not available to people of color.

My parents told me and my brothers and sisters—there were nine of us in all—that we were as good as anybody, regardless of our skin color. But what they said conflicted with what we saw and experienced. Symbols can have a profound effect upon young, developing minds. Symbols and images speak louder than words. The symbols, images, and barriers to which we were exposed were sanctioned by unjust laws. In effect, they said that one group was inferior and the other group superior. As a result, both groups became slaves to a myth that manifested itself in hatred, atrocities, murder, and the imprisonment of the mind.

When Dr. King came on the scene, he rekindled hope where "hope unborn had died." He articulated the effects these barriers, images, and symbols had on individuals. Under his leadership the visible symbols, images, and barriers were removed. His message was: "you are somebody." He told the nation that the American creed should be extended to include all its citizens: "We hold these truths to be self-evident that all men are created equal; that they are endowed by their Creator with certain inalienable rights; that among these are life, liberty, and the pursuit of happiness."

Dr. King had a dream, a dream rooted in the American dream. I, like so many people of color, got caught up in that dream; indeed, the whole nation and maybe the whole world got caught up in that dream. It is the motivating force behind my candidacy for city council. My inspiration is fueled by the memory of my brother Oneal, who was killed by night riders in 1965 because he had the audacity to pursue his dream. It provides the courage and puts the fire in my belly.

Oneal, in 1964, realized his dream of becoming a deputy sheriff in Varnado, Louisiana. He was beaming with pride over his accomplishment when I visited him in April of 1965. I jokingly said to him, "Show me your tin badge." He said nothing but left the room. He returned in a few moments fully dressed in his uniform. He pointed to his badge and said, "This ain't no tin badge." In June 1965, he was killed by night riders. But he still realized his dream although it was short-lived. We, individually, must have the courage to pursue our dreams. Perhaps just as important, we need dreams to pursue. But I have a nobler purpose in aspiring to be a city councilman. I want to help make the city I love a better place to live. I have a dream for this city, a vision. I have a vision that this city will be a model city in the state of California. A city with the highest rate of employment; a city with the highest per capita income; a city with adequate affordable housing; a city where the emphasis is on education—the best education obtainable—from Head Start through graduate school; a city with the lowest crime rate; a city with the best police force money can provide, but a force that respects the rights of all citizens and enforces the law equally, without abuse, among all groups; a city that provides opportunity for its youth to realize their dreams regardless of what they might be. I have a vision of a vibrant, bustling city; a city that is the industrial and cultural leader in the Inland Empire.

My wife and I arrived in this city in 1960 with our oldest son Jeff. I was a starving young air force sergeant, but we survived. We had two more sons here in the city of Riverside: Steve and Carl. We now have two grandchildren: a boy and a girl. Stephen Ameal is three years old and Lindsay Charee is one year old. I want those kids and kids of their generation to grow up in a safe, happy environment, an environment where the symbols and role models are conducive for them to develop their full potential and live the American dream.

This is my hope. This is my dream. This is the motivating force behind my candidacy. I invite all of you to support me. Together, let's make the vision I have shared with you tonight a reality.

The Campaign

The first thing we did was open an office in the shopping center on the east side of Chicago Avenue. The owner of the center leased the space to me as a donation to my campaign. My campaign office was very visible in the community, and interested or curious people could drop by anytime during the day. My slogan was: "Will Deliver, ready to serve." This slogan came to mind from the Postal Service's unofficial motto: "Neither snow nor rain nor heat nor gloom of night stays these couriers from the swift completion of their appointed rounds."

One day a gentleman by the name of Bill Dole, a real estate agent with the firm of Armstrong Realtors, stopped by my headquarters. He introduced himself and said he would like to assist in my campaign. Wow! I believe what Bill did for me in the Canyon Crest area won the election. Bill knew personally just about every family in the area and went door-to-door with me, urging them to support my candidacy. They did, and we won the election.

Another individual that walked the Canyon Crest area with me was Harry Hood. He went door-to-door with me and presented me in a very positive light. He urged many people to support my candidacy. It was excited, and everyone's support motivated me I could see myself in the position of councilman and had fire in my belly and in my bones.

Two other individuals—members of Second Baptist Church—that walked portions of the Second Ward with/for me were David Chandler and Mitchell A. Curtis.

There were five candidates in total, including former Mayor Ab Brown. Still, I felt positive. At candidate forums, Ab had gotten into the habit of saying that he was not running against me and the other candidates; he said he was running against city hall. After a while, I had my fill of this rhetoric and told Ab at one of these forums: "You are not running against city hall: you are running against me."

The election that November ended in a runoff, as none of us received 50 percent of the vote. Ab Brown and I were the two top candidates and ended up in a runoff election in January 1994.

This was a bit of a challenge. I wanted to stay in contact with potential voters in the ward without interrupting their holidays. Dottie (my campaign manager) and I came up with the idea of a family photo that would include Henrietta and me but would feature my sons and their wives, along with my grandchildren. We had the photo made into holiday Greeting cards and mailed them to every registered voter in the Second Ward. It was very impressive. The feedback I received later indicated that our effort touched our constituents emotionally. As I said earlier, we won the runoff election by a comfortable margin, 60 percent of the vote.

Attempted Recall

Approximately a year after the election, I was one among three council members subjected to a recall: Second Ward (me), Fourth Ward (Maureen Kane), and Sixth Ward (Terry Thompson).

The mayor's Salary Commission, which consisted of representatives from each ward (seven in total) recommended to increase the council members' salary by 19 percent. The council approved the recommended increase. Now, 19 percent sounds like a lot, but when you are only receiving a small stipend, the increase didn't amount to a lot of money and was not unreasonable. Besides, it had been years since the council had received a salary increase.

I must admit up front that I did not run for office because of the salary; I ran for office because I wanted to serve the constituents in the Second Ward and the city of Riverside. However, I did not know how much time my work would come to demand. It seems that I and my colleagues attended a meeting or work-related social gathering most evenings each week.

Mr. Jones, a military retiree and, if I remember correctly, "a triple dipper"—military, social security and Medicare—led a group determined to recall the three most recently elected council members from the second, fourth, and sixth wards.

It was with mixed emotions that I faced this potential recall—anger and fear. I was angry because I thought the recall was unfair; fearful because I thought they might be successful in their attempt.

I have always felt that my election to the council was a blessing and a gift from the Lord—the fulfillment of that still, soft voice that had told me many years earlier it had "something special" for me. I began questioning the Lord about what was happening. I said to the Almighty, "Are you going to let them recall me before I have served a year in office? I am here because of you."

The anger in me led me to fight the recall attempt along with my colleagues Maureen Kane and Terry Thompson. The three of us put up a powerful defense. Well, the Almighty must have heard my prayers and intervened because Mr. Jones—the leader of the group—died, and the rest of the group dropped the recall effort. Shortly afterward, an Riverside Unified School District RUSD Trustee—the attorney Joseph

Peters Myers—approached me and Henrietta in Costco and quipped, "Boy, you had better not mess with the city council; you might end up dead."

I would serve twelve years—three terms—on the council; they were the most exciting years of my life, a dream fulfilled.

Pursue your dream; work hard and keep your eyes on your goal—it adds so much more meaning to life, and your legacy will serve to motivate others.

Trip to China

In 1996, I was a city councilman and led an International Relations Council (IRC) Delegation to Wujiang City, China. Rose Oliver, an involved, well-respected individual in the community made the arrangement. The IRC and the city council work very closely together. In fact, the Mayor ad I both were members. The IRC fosters goodwill between the USA and other countries around the world. Of course, Rose Oliver was a member in good standing with the IRC as were most of us. Other members included representatives from UCR (University of California, Riverside) and the local *Wall Street Journal* (WSJ) distribution center as well.

We took an eight or nine hour flight from LAX to Japan and then to China. A police escort met us at the airport and escorted us to our hotel in Wujiang City. We received the red carpet treatment at the hotel when we arrived; the beautifully attired young Chinese girls flanked the entrance on both sides. Following formal greetings and a midnight snack (we had arrived at approximately 11 p.m.); we were escorted to our rooms and bedded down for the night.

Our purpose in coming to China was to consider naming Wujiang City as our sister city.

The next day began a whirlwind tour of manufacturing plants and garment districts throughout the city. In addition, we saw several new construction projects throughout the city. The manufacturing sector was obviously growing and looking for the opportunity to market its products.

It was an adventure to ride a small tour bus in China; at least that was the case with us. The driver would pass the vehicle in front of him without any regard for opposing traffic. While we thought we were headed for a head-on collision, the drivers would swerve at the last moment. Wow! What an adventure.

We spent a day and a night in Shanghai, China, a city about thirty miles west of Wujiang City. Shanghai is a beautiful city with dragon gardens and lots of bicycles. I have never seen so many bicycles in all my life. Bicycles seemed to be the major mode of transportation in Shanghai and throughout that part of China as a whole.

The waterfront of Shanghai is very modern. To me, it had a western atmosphere. In the ocean, but in sight of the coast, about three hundred feet there was a beautiful building that bore this encryption: "The Pearl of the Orient." I assume it means that Shanghai is the pearl of the orient.

We had a delicious dinner in Shanghai where I practiced using chopsticks. After some practice, I did fairly well. It was, however, a bit disconcerting to see, upon entering our restaurant, a snake in a cage (possibly a rattle snake). Was a snake included in our dinner? I don't know, but I/we enjoyed the dinner nonetheless.

The one thing that still stands out in my mind about China was the lack of idleness. Everyone seemed to be busy doing something—sweeping the streets, working in rice patties, doing construction work, manufacturing, selling etc.

Every night after we returned to Wujiang City, the day's tour ended with a delicious dinner. Our hosts usually drank a great deal at these dinners; they drowned in liquor. I recall a statement made by the American ambassador for the area. He said, "I have sacrificed my liver for the good of my country." There may be more truth in that statement than we would want to admit.

In addition to touring factories and plants, we were treated to an amusement park full of children and their parents. But it was nothing compared to Disneyland as we know it in California. The main thing though, was to see kids and their families enjoying themselves.

The day before we departed for our return to the US, I had the honor and the privilege of addressing the mayor and the council in Wujiang City. I thanked them for their hospitality and their interest in becoming a sister city to Riverside. However, I emphasized that the final decision would be made by the Riverside city council. Ultimately the council approved Jung Ming instead of Wujiang City.

That night after dinner, we performed for our hosts. Rose Oliver had arranged for our delegation to sing some familiar songs as well as dance to entertain our hosts. It turned out very well—much better than I had anticipated. I was scared to death but was able to mask it.

All-America City

1 998 was an eventful year, a roller-coaster year. Some of my recollections include All-America City; a trip to South Africa; a shooting at city hall; and the killing of Tyisha Miller—a Black teenage girl—by Riverside police.

The year started out on a high note: Riverside was designated an All-America City by the National Civic League. This is quite an achievement, as there are a lot of cities competing for this award.

The criteria for this designation were all inclusive. The awards committee was looking for cities with low crime rates, recreation facilities, educational institutions, as well as sports and youth programs. Therefore, to be designated an All-America City is to be celebrated. In the 1998 All-America City Yearbook, former senator Bill Bradley states: "The people who participated in the 1998 City Awards are all winners. They are winners because they realize that hope begins at home when one person calls another person, who talks to a neighbor who calls someone else to ask if they want to join in a collective effort to make the community a better place. They are winners because they have learned the most important lesson—the importance of giving to someone else with no expectation of return."

We celebrated by sending a delegation back to Mobile, Alabama. Unfortunately I was not among the delegates, but our delegation kept us informed by telephone. The delegation participated in contests, programs, and social events; it was a festive, happy occasion, and we were a proud city. Council members, I believe, were proudest of all. After all, as elected officials, we represented the people. We felt we were instrumental in helping put the city in a position to compete for this award. The city of Riverside was among the top ten cities in the nation to receive the All-America City Award in1998.

South Africa

In August 1998, councilman Charles (Chuck) Beaty and I led a delegation to South Africa, which Rose Oliver, with the aid of Norm Martin, arranged. At that time, Martin was the health administrator (CEO) at Parkview Hospital and had been to South Africa several times. Rose Oliver arranged the trip on behalf of the International Relations Council (IRC), which sought a sister city in South Africa.

Norm Martin had already whetted my interest for South Africa with his description of it. He compared its topography and climate to that of Southern California. All my life I had wanted to visit Africa, the birthplace of my ancestors, so it was with great excitement and anticipation that I looked forward to the trip.

The delegation flew out of LAX to Miami and boarded a nonstop flight to Cape Town, South Africa. We flew South Africa Airlines (SAA); we had a fifteen-hour nonstop flight. I was so excited that the length of the flight didn't bother me on the way there, but it was more difficult on the return trip because I was a bit anxious to get back home.

After landing at the airport in Cape Town, we were bused to our hotel, which was very nice. Chuck and I were roommates throughout our trip. The next morning we woke early and went for a walk. We began each day this way except when we spent the night at a nature reserve in tree houses.

When we boarded the tour bus that first morning, we traveled to Table Mountain, which provides a panoramic view of Cape Town and its surroundings. From Table Mountain, we had a clear view of Robben Island, the island where Nelson Mandela was imprisoned for eighteen years.

I am not always comfortable with heights. To get to the top of Table Mountain, we had to travel by cable car, and the ascent was quite steep. To reduce my fear, I positioned myself in the middle of the delegation and engaged myself in conversation until we reached the top—it was worth the effort. It was a spectacular view of the area.

When we came down from Table Mountain and toured the waterfront area, which consisted of restaurants and entertainment clubs. The Hard Rock Café that we saw there was bombed the very next evening. We had planned to visit the area again and have dinner, but after touring the winery, we were exhausted and decided not to do so. Was Providence guiding us?

The next day's tour of the winery and other places of interest on the northwest side of Cape Town (a rural area), proved very interesting: we learned how they made their wine and saw the facilities as well as the neighboring. As Norm Martin had described, the topography, climate, and overall look resembles Southern California.

After a long, exhausting day, we returned to our hotel in Cape Town, but instead of going down to the waterfront as planned, we bedded down for the night. The next morning, we received news that there had been a bombing at one of the restaurants we had planned to visit. A reporter interviewed Chuck Beaty concerning the incident and its effect on us.

From the waterfront, we boarded a boat and sailed for a tour of Robben Island. What an interesting tour. We saw the quarry where the prisoners worked daily, the small cramped cell where Nelson Mandela spent the first eighteen years of his twenty-seven-year imprisonment, the cafeteria, and recreational area. I, for one, left the island with a greater appreciation of Mandela, who I had already greatly admired.

The next day, our tour included a park overlooking the ocean. We saw a beautiful view of the area. However, what I experienced before and after going to the top of the hill was even more interesting.

While standing in the parking lot observing the baboons present there, I noticed some baboons entering the open windows of the buses parked there. They were taking the food that tourists had left on the buses. They would then sit on the hoods of parked cars and enjoy their good fortune, even Kentucky Fried Chicken and other fast food. I could not believe my eyes, so I took pictures to convince the skeptics I would encounter later. I thought baboons ate bananas and other fruit, but Kentucky Fried Chicken? You have to be kidding me! But it happened.

The next city we visited was Durbin, which is a seaside city on the eastside of South Africa. We flew up to Durbin and only spent a few hours there; we saw most of the city from our tour bus.

Leaving Durbin for a nature reserve, our tour bus broke down at an intersection about the time school let out. We all sat quietly on the bus and waited for the replacement to arrive; the number of kids at the intersection was growing.

I decided to get off the bus and greet the kids. I got off the bus, shook hands with the kids, and engaged them in conversation. Soon, most of the delegation joined me in interacting with the children. Shortly afterward, the police arrived and advised us to get back on the bus, and we did as they advised.

I was very comfortable interacting with those kids and felt right at home. I said to my colleague and good friend Chuck, "Who knows? I might return here and run for office."

We boarded a replacement bus, drove to a nature reserve, had dinner, and saw a performance by native Africans dancers. Leaving the reserve, we boarded the tour bus and traveled to Pietermaritzburg, a college town in the northeast area of South Africa.

We spent the next couple days in Pietermaritzburg touring the campus and meeting college officials. Pietermaritzburg was beginning to show potential as a sister city: it was a college town, and so was Riverside; its population was about three hundred thousand, and so was Riverside's. The next day, when we drove up on the mountain overlooking the city, we found that the topography and the climate were similar to Riverside's.

Our hotel room in Pietermaritzburg must have had the largest free-standing bathtub I have ever seen. I thought I was going to have to call Chuck to help me get out of the tub.

The first morning we were in Pietermaritzburg and took our early morning walk, Chuck and I came upon a statue of Mahatma Gandhi. The statue commemorated an act of violence: Gandhi was thrown off a train in South Africa. The inscription read: "Great men suffer indignities that—projected into the future—make the equality of life better for the natives."

Leaving Pietermaritzburg, our tour guide took us to a nature reserve where we spent the day observing wild animals. I believe we saw every species except elephants, lions, and tigers. That evening after dinner, we spent the night in tree houses, which were about five to six feet above ground. We slept under mosquito nets and could see and hear the animals in the reserve. It was a very exciting experience, one that I remember fondly.

Moving on, our next stop was in Pretoria, the seat of government in South Africa. We spent a night and a day in Pretoria, a very clean city, meeting with governmental officials. Now that I think about it, what I remember most is that the officials were rarely on time.

The final city we visited was Johannesburg. Johannesburg is the largest city in South Africa, and like most of the cities we visited, the native Africans were confined to the outskirts of the city in overcrowded conditions. But optimism was in the air. Apartheid had ended. Nelson Mandela was president, and the future looked very promising.

I remember the delegation going to a nice restaurant in Johannesburg where ostrich was on the menu. I decided to give it a try and ordered it for dinner. It wasn't bad. Chuck was not as adventurous and ordered something more familiar.

The highlight of our visit to Johannesburg was the dinner we had in the home of a resident there. She lived in a nice, "matchbox house" (small), which was being expanded while we had dinner there. Our host—I wish I could remember her name—was very gracious. She worked for the government and spoke several different languages. She was very careful that we were comfortable and served her best wine with the delicious meal she had prepared.[1]

The other highlight was the tour of Nelson and Winnie Mandela's home. The tour guide there was an individual with a striking resemblance to Officer Jim Cannon of the

---

[1]   match

Riverside Police Department. When we came back, Chuck and I told Jim, "We know where you migrated from; we saw one of your relatives in South Africa."

We also saw Bishop Tutu's home and, I believe, a church under his jurisdiction. I was disappointed, and I believe the rest of the delegation was as well, that we didn't get to meet or see Nelson Mandela or Bishop Desmond Tutu in person.

Well, it was a wonderful trip, but after ten days it was time to return home to the USA. It is a trip I will always remember with fondness. I cannot adequately describe how relaxed and at home I felt in South Africa. It was déjà vu.

We boarded a South Africa Airline (SAA) flight out of Johannesburg, refueled on the coast of West Africa, and landed back in the USA at JFK airport in New York.

I was so exhausted when we landed at JFK that I started up the downstairs escalator. Later it made me think of the plight of my people: we have been climbing the downstairs escalator all our lives; those of us that walk faster than the escalator coming down reach the top; those that don't work all their lives and seemingly make little or no progress.

Shooting at City Hall

After being elected to city council, one of the first things I and the newly elected mayor—Ronald Loveridge—got involved in was an attempt to reinstate Joseph Neal in his former position of teaching chess at Bordwell Park. The mayor and I met with Joe Neal and listened to his explanation of the value of teaching young minority kids to play chess. We then arranged a meeting with the manager of the park's facility—Jeanie Williams—to try to persuade her to reinstate Joe Neal. Ms Williams said, "Absolutely not; he doesn't follow instructions." After that meeting, we discontinued our efforts.

Shortly afterward, Joe Neal served a subpoena to the mayor, city manager, and other city employees (including me) to appear and testify before an administrative law judge. Joe Neal lost his attempt to get reinstated, as the judge upheld the dismissal. Thus began Joe Neal's regular attendance at city council meetings every Tuesday. He was very visible in the audience but said nothing. The one thing that he did do on a regular basis was write letters to decision-makers in the community, such as the school superintendent, county supervisors, the governor, and city council members (at least to me). His complaint, in a nutshell, was the city's treatment of minorities. He wrote passionately on this topic.

On a few occasions, during a break in the council meetings, I would talk to Joe Neal. He was very fond of his mother and grandmother and appeared to be greatly influenced by them. In the letters I received from him—and I received many—he often mentioned them. I never realized how bitter and angry he was over his dismissal from Bordwell Park.

On October 6, 1998, all hell broke loose. My colleague and close friend Chuck Beaty, the First Ward councilman, and I went into city hall and walked downstairs to the council chambers. There stood Joe Neal, holding a briefcase on the ledge near the front entrance. We greeted him, as we were accustomed to seeing him at council meetings. Chuck and I said, "Hi Joe," but whether or not he returned the greeting, I don't recall. Chuck and I proceeded to the closed session room of the chambers, where we always found doughnuts and coffee. Not more than five minutes later, Joe Neal burst into the room. He didn't say a word and began firing away with a 9 mm pistol.

At first I thought it was the sound of firecrackers going off until I saw Joe with the gun. Alex Clifford (Fifth Ward), the mayor, and I ducked for cover under the large table in the middle of the room. Alex ducked under the table but continued out the rear door. The mayor and I lay side by side quietly watching the event unfold. Chuck Beaty and Laura Pierson (Seventh Ward councilwoman) tackled Joe Neal in an attempt to disarm him; he pistol-whipped Laura and shot Chuck Beaty point-blank three times. At the rear of the room, near the phone and rear door, lay Terry Thompson (Sixth Ward councilwoman); I thought she was dead, and I thought the same thing about Laura Pierson (Seventh Ward councilwoman), who lay quietly near the front door. John Holmes—the city manager—appeared at the rear door as Chuck staggered out of the room. John immediately called for help and aided Chuck until medical and the fire department arrived and dispatched Chuck to the emergency room at Community Hospital, a half-mile from city hall. In the mean time, Joe Neal was writing something on the chalk board on the south wall while the mayor and I lay side by side under the table. That familiar still, soft voice said to me, "Be quiet; you are going to be okay."

Joe Neal had bolted the front door to the conference room and as I have said, was writing something on the chalkboard behind us. Then he began pulling the mayor and me out from under the table. Shots rang out at the front door—the police had arrived. Joe Neal returned fire at the door, wounding Wally Rice, one of the officers. The police wounded Laura Pierson in the hip. Eventually the police was able to take down Joe Neal and rescue us—Terry Thompson, Laura Pierson, the mayor, and me. All this happened within fifteen minutes, but it seemed like a lifetime. The mayor sustained a flesh wound to his back, and a bullet grazed the sleeve of my coat.

I will return to this event in a later chapter.

The Shooting of Tyisha Miller

A 911 call by Riverside police officers for medical assistance for a young girl found asleep or unconscious in an automobile took place on the night of December 28, 1998. At the time this would appear to be a humanitarian gesture but what unfolded turned out to be barbarism in my opinion.

When Police Chief Jerry Carroll called me the morning of December 28, 1998 and told me about the shooting and death of Tyisha Miller, I was shocked. Very few facts were known at that time. The chief said he would like to have a meeting with community leaders, and I willingly assisted him in compiling a list of names consisting of: the clergy, heads of community-based organizations (CBOs), and other community leaders and citizens.

Once at the meeting, the chief briefed us with the known facts of the incident. All of us present agreed that the available information was insufficient to determine what prompted the shooting and that we should wait for further investigation to reveal the facts. (I believe they knew more than they cared to share at the time but wanted to make sure the public did not over react).

However, when the autopsy report came back from the sheriff's department on December 31, 1998 revealing that Ms. Miller had been shot twelve times, I was outraged. Ms. Miller had received four gunshot wounds to the head; five to the back; one to the chest; one to the upper right arm; and one to the left thigh.

I have no idea what could have prompted those police officers to fire as many as twenty-eight shots. Remember, the 911 call was for medical assistance, and the officers found Tyisha either asleep or unconscious. A thorough, complete, and impartial investigation needed to be completed at once, and the people responsible needed to be made accountable.

This is not a condemnation of the Riverside Police Department. I think we have one of the best in the nation. I have seen them at their finest. In October of the same year, they rescued us from Joe Neal at city hall. This incident showed me the officers at their worst; I believe their poor judgment took a young girl's life.

Justice must be done, and I think it will be done when all the facts are known. No one is above the law. When officers have the authority to be judge, jury, and executioner, they must be held responsible for their actions.

Chief Jerry Carroll was the right man at the right time to deal with this situation. He met with the clergy and the demonstrators regularly and took steps to remove the four officers responsible for the killing of Tyisha Miller. These were courageous steps, as the Chief was under a lot of pressure to support those officers. It cost him his job, but I strongly feel that he did the right thing.

My congratulations and thanks go out to the clergy: Reverends Jerry Louder, Paul Munford, L. E. Campbell, Jesse Wilson, and other whose names I no longer remember. Their cool heads and organization helped us to avoid any potential violence.

The Reverends Jesse Jackson and Al Sharpton came out and brought national attention to the incident and gave strength and encouragement to the demonstrators. As a councilman, I was not supportive of their presence in Riverside, but I do believe they had a positive effect. They both were/are well known civil rights leaders throughout the nation and for the most part respected. Their presence, I believe, said to responsible individuals (especially the Chief of Police) do what is right in this situation.

Finally I would like to say, thank you, Chief Jerry Carroll. You are a good and decent man. I have great respect for you and the action you took in dealing with this incident. God bless you.

Accomplishments

I look back with a deep sense of pride and satisfaction at the many things we accomplished during my twelve years as councilman of the second ward. We revitalized University Avenue. We created a new streetscape complete with decorative medians; we demolished old motels and erected new buildings and bus shelters. In collaboration with the University of California Riverside (UCR), we established University Village which gave rebirth to University Avenue from UCR to downtown.

I consider University Village to be the centerpiece University Avenue's revitalization. It provided both students and community members with movie theaters, restaurants, fast food, video games, additional classrooms in the theaters and, finally, Riverside's first Starbucks.

Riverside's first Starbucks is an interesting story. Michael Beck, an employee at UCR (who later worked for the city)Michael worked out of the office of Vice chancellor Jim Erickson and was greatly responsible for the Galas In the Desert that I will tell you about in a later chapter; negotiated with Starbucks to bring a store to University Village. Starbucks looked at the demographics of the area and concluded it would not be profitable because the village was located on the east side of town, a low-income area. Michael finally persuaded them to build the store, arguing that the demographics were misleading. He/we believed that if there was a Starbucks in University Village, then people would go to it. In its first year, Starbucks became the highest grossing store in its region. A year or so later, University Village received its second Starbucks, located down the street on the corner of University and Iowa Avenues. Now we have two locations and counting.

In the 1970s and early 1980s, Riverside Raceway was located where Moreno Valley Mall is now situated, and there were motels all along University Avenue that provided lodging for race fans and participants. The motels brought in money to the city and thrived. However, when the raceway closed, the motels became sites of prostitution; they turned into an eyesore to the community. The police station at University Village never had a dull moment, especially on weekends.

In 1994, when I was elected to city council and Ron Loveridge was elected mayor, we later made it our goal to get rid of the blight along University Avenue. As of this writing, there are only three remaining motels.

The Marketplace is another area of which I am very proud. Councilman Jack Clarke Sr., Riverside's first Black city councilman (1986-1993) initiated the project. It's a thriving area with restaurants, a Metrolink station, a bank, a photo studio and real estate offices. With the help of the Redevelopment Department, a much-blighted area got a new look and a very promising future.

Prior to the construction of University Village, Raceway Ford, which was located near the corner of Iowa and Linden streets, moved to Sycamore Canyon and the 60 Freeway. They experienced a sales increase of 20 percent the first year at their new location. Needless to say, I was very proud of the results. In fact, Sycamore Canyon—Riverside's industrial area—was just starting to be developed. By the time I left office in February 2006, it was at least 75-80 percent complete. Also located in the Sycamore Canyon area is Sycamore Canyon Neighborhood Park, of which I am extremely proud. It is located at the top of the Sycamore Canyon Wilderness Park and affords a panoramic view of the entire area.

Sycamore Canyon contained a new housing development area with land designated for a park but without adequate funds to construct it. Terry Nielsen, the director of the Parks and Recreation Department, informed me that they had about half the funds (five hundred thousand dollars) appropriated but would need an additional five hundred thousand to complete construction. I asked if the additional funds needed were in his budget, and he replied that they were. Other wards (example, ward four) shared in the generation of these funds and could object to using the funds for this perpose.

At the next council meeting, there was an agenda item for funding Sycamore Canyon Neighborhood Park. I moved that Parks and Recreation fund the park in the amount of one million dollars, which would allow them to complete the construction. The motion was seconded and unanimously approved! The residents in the audience were euphoric; it was a surreal moment for me.

I am also pleased with the revitalization of the Chicago Avenue Shopping Center, located at University and Chicago Avenues and extending south to Eleventh Street. For years, the shopping center located on the west side of Chicago Avenue had been deteriorating. I, with the help of the Development Department, worked for years to bring in a big box development, such as Walmart. This never materialized. Finally, a new owner purchased the property, rehabbed old buildings, and added new ones. It gave the shopping center a new birth. It is now bustling with shoppers!

My work on city bus shelters was not as successful as my other accomplishments. From 1998-2006, I was a board member of Riverside Transit Agency (RTA). I replaced Alex Clifford, a councilman from the Fifth Ward, when he left the city council in 1998. While on the board, I pursued the project to replace city bus shelters. Riverside summers are hot—the temperature is often in the triple digits. In that heat, it's very uncomfortable for customers to stand outside and wait for the bus. There were several ad agencies willing to provide and maintain air conditioned shelters at no cost to the city or RTA if they could place ads on the shelters. To me, this was a no-brainer, especially since the city council would have the opportunity to determine which ads were appropriate.

I was successful in getting this item onto the council agenda. When it came up for consideration, I explained to the council that an ad agency would provide shelters at no cost to the city in exchange for free advertising (which the city would approve). The item was approved unanimously. However, I left the council in February 2006, and the project never proceeded. Evidently pressure on the council from city elites—non-bus riders—prevented the project's implementation. No council member since has come forward to push for bus shelters, and I am very disappointed. Working individuals who do not have their own transportation depend upon RTA to go back and forth to work, shopping, doctor's appointments, and recreational activities; bus shelters should be provided for them. Maybe the escalating price of gasoline will get lower middle-class workers out of their cars and onto the buses. The population needs to apply pressure to city council to provide bus shelters for a growing population of riders.

Another project, the Orange Blossom Festival, was discontinued after ten years because of (at least, I suspect) complaints from the downtown business community. The Orange Blossom Festival was one of Riverside's signature events for the city. It had begun based on the recommendation of John Husing, PhD, one of the top economists in Southern California and possibly the entire state. It was implemented in 1995 and discontinued in 2005. At one time, Riverside was the citrus capital of the Inland Empire. The Orange Blossom Festival intended to commemorate this period in the city's history. We celebrated it with a parade led by a horse-drawn carriage and men and women in period dress: men wore tuxedos and top hats, and women dressed in beautiful long dresses, some with parasols. There were displays commemorating the period throughout the downtown area. The kickoff was—in the early days of the festival—at the Mission Inn, where we gathered in formal attire to commemorate the period and enjoyed refreshments.

Evidently the downtown merchants and city elites wanted to discontinue the festival based on a few incidents of rowdiness that occurred after dark. I believe these incidents could have been eliminated or reduced by closing down the festivities by six o'clock instead of eight or nine o'clock. In any event, if you really want something, you will find a way to keep it going; if you do not want it, you look for an excuse to shoot it down. I think the city made a mistake in discontinuing the Orange Blossom Festival, and I hope that it will be reinstated sometime in the near future.

My Mom

My mom was born in Tunica, Louisiana, the second child in a family of four children—two girls and two boys. The girls' names were: Mary Day (Smothers) and Margaret Ann (Smothers; my mom); the boys' names were: Arthur (Wilson) and Daniel (Smothers). The boys both had nicknames: Arthur's nickname was "Black." Ironically this nickname was the opposite of his skin color; he was a very light-skinned individual. Daniel's nickname was "Catfish" and "Nony." I have no idea to what "Nony" referred.

Their parents were Mary (Webb) and Sterling Smothers. Mom loved her dad, Sterling Smothers, and talked about him frequently to us. I am sure she loved her mom also, but she talked most about her dad.

Mom was raised in West Feliciana, Louisiana, near Angola prison. She said she could see the prison from where she lived. At a family reunion in 2006, I had the opportunity to drive up to Angola prison with my sisters Vera Mae Bullock and Elizabeth Daniels. The prison was about fifteen to twenty miles from where the reunion was held. It brought back memories of Mom and gave me a glimpse of her experience growing up.

Mom loved to talk and tell us stories she had read: the three pigs; the story of Hansel and Gretel; the stroll; the bunny rabbit in Mr. McGregor's garden; and the one about the father and son on their way to the market—just to mention a few.

I don't recall Mom mentioning any work she did outside the house when she was growing up or as an adult. One thing we knew she was determined not to do was to work in some White person's kitchen, and to my knowledge, she never did.

Born and raised in the segregated South, I would get awful nervous accompanying my mom shopping. She would find a dress she liked, and, because Colored folks were not allowed to try on clothes, Mom would not buy it. Not only would she not buy it, she would also say it was a piece of junk. This was what happened when we went shopping in Poplarville, Mississippi. For the most part, Mom bought her clothing in Bogalusa, Louisiana. Even though Bogalusa was a segregated city also, Mom evidently was allowed to try on the clothes she bought there.

Mom had some pretty legs. This feature must have been dominant in her genes because she passed it down to all of her daughters and granddaughters, even to some of her sons and grandsons. There was a saying in our town that when someone had beautiful legs, "You must be related to Margaret Moore."

Mom had a beautiful singing voice, and she often sang solos at church. She also sang at home while doing housework or to cope with something that was bothering her. I particularly enjoyed hearing Mom sing two songs: "Precious Lord" and "Amazing Grace." She sang them with so much feeling and passion that they would bring tears to your eyes, and many in the congregation were *inclined to shout* their appreciation. Even today when I hear a good soloist or an instrumentalist play those songs, I can't hold back the tears because they bring back memories of Mom.

Mom's mother was a beautiful fair-skinned woman. Her name was Mary Etta Webb. In December of 2010, I acquired a picture of her during a Christmas visit with my siblings and relatives in Mississippi. I could not see her legs, but I would bet they were pretty like Mom's. I'm sure that Mom inherited them from her.

Prior to meeting Dad—Stephen (Steve) Moore—Mom had had three children in a previous marriage to Robert Johnson. They were Iberville, Leola, and Curtis Johnson.

Dad had a son, Caldwell Moore, by a previous relationship, though I don't know the mother's name. In fact, Dad had an older son, whose name is Pressie, by his first wife, Eola. As of this writing, Pressie lives in Mobile, Alabama and is in his nineties. Pressie is the spitting image of our dad. We had never seen a child resemble a parent to the extent that Pressie resembles Dad. I was fascinated by how much they resembled each other.

I don't know the type of work Mom's dad did; I believe he was a tailor or shoe salesman, or maybe both. In any event, she enjoyed following him around. Mom loved fish. It didn't matter about the size as long as it was a fish. As a teenager, my brother Oneal used this knowledge to his advantage when he stayed out later than permitted on dates. He was supposed to be home between ten and eleven o'clock. When he was late, he would bring mom a fish sandwich, and whatever discipline she may have had in mind was put aside or forgotten.

When my brother Oneal was ambushed and killed in June 1965, it penetrated her soul and broke her heart. She did not attend Oneal's funeral; it was too much for her to bear. Of course Dad was there with Oneal's widow Mavella and family, and they shared each other's pain and sorrow as did the Moore family as a whole. In a pamphlet titled "Free At Last", published by Southern Poverty Law Center in Montgomery, Alabama, Mavella's mother is mistakenly identified in a photo at the grave site as Dad's wife.

Mom never did recover from this incident; she died many years later with a broken heart. There was no closure for her; no one was ever brought to trial for the crime, and it continued to be an open sore for the entire family.

Dad was born in Demopolis, Alabama. His father's name was Joe (Joseph) Moore; his mother's name was Clarab. There were six siblings: Forest, Essex, Stephen (Dad) Mary J., Lena, and Ellen. Three other names are listed on the 1910 census—Roscom James, Mary James, and Lilly James, but I don't know their relationship to my father's family. I met Aunt Ellen when she came out to California to visit her son Eddie Carter, in Los Angeles, in the mid 1970s. She was a dark-skinned lady with round shoulders like my dad's. She and Eddie came to visit us in Riverside, California when we lived on Wroxton Drive. I really enjoyed their visit, and I learned a bit more about our family's history.

I met Aunt Selena (Lena) and Uncle Essex on several occasions while growing up in White Sand, Mississippi. I suppose it was an instant love affair; I thought they were both charming. My sisters Elizabeth and Vera Mae must have inherited their beautiful hair.

Dad was a deacon in our family's church—New Welcome Baptist Church. Dad was a very devout Christian, and he taught the adult Sunday school class. His attendance at the church was perfect. He was a no-nonsense individual; oh, he had a good sense of humor, but profanity really turned him off. He must have thought profanity was evidence of a small mind. The closest I ever heard him come to using profanity was "aw-shucks."

Dad was the church treasurer for as long as I can remember. He was very thorough and accurate in accounting. Tithes were referred to as dues, and all church members were expected to pay their dues.

My dad was also the community barber—he cut the hair and shaved the beards of the men in the community. This was before we had electricity, so Dad operated the clippers by hand. He was good at it.

I remember one year, Dad and Mom hosted the preacher who did the revival at New Welcome Baptist Church. His name was Reverend Black and he spent the week of revival with us. I was thirteen or fourteen years old but a little runt. Reverend Black said to me one night as we sat on the porch, "Boy, do you want to grow?" I said, "Yes sir." He told me, "You need to get out in the field and plow and you will grow."

That spring and summer, I farmed our 10 acres, applying the techniques I learned in my agriculture class at school, and produced a bumper crop of corn. Believe it or not, I grew just like the corn. Over the next several years, I experienced a growth spurt. Reverend Black was right—the physical exercise involved in plowing caused me to grow.

My dad could play the harmonica; we called it the "juice harp." The only thing I remember him playing was "The Train," with a full head of steam moving down the tracks and blowing its whistle at railroad crossings. Dad said it took a lot of physical energy to play some tunes, and therefore he did not do it very often.

I remember Dad telling about an incident from his Sunday school class. He said as he stood before the class, he began by searching for his reading glasses. He looked in his shirt pocket and his coat pocket; finally someone in the class—Desline Travis—asked, "What are you looking for, Brother Steve?"

"My glasses", Dad replied.

"You have them on", replied Sister Travis. Dad would break out in laughter whenever he told that story. You see, he did have a sense of humor.

I loved my dad. He would walk the distance from White Sand to Poplarville—ten miles round trip—just to get me a can of pork and beans. Growing up, I loved pork and beans. I loved Dad to the point that when he died and I was not at his bedside, I had to go to a psychiatrist to deal with the guilt. The psychiatrist suggested I write a letter to my dad. Below is what I wrote, and it relieved me of my guilt:

Dear Dad,

I am sorry I was not by your bedside when you died. I think I would have liked to have held your hand and told you how much I loved you. Of all the people in my life, it is you that I loved most. You have always been so kind and benevolent toward me; you trusted me and placed in my hands the responsibility for and the division of your assets. I am sorry I could not or was not there when you needed me most—when you were put into the hospital in Poplarville, Mississippi and you asked where I was.

Forgive me, Dad, for my shortcomings and my cowardice. I wish I could be the man you were. You were a man of strong convictions and stood up for what you believed. May your spirit and your memory forever be with me.

Thank you so much for all that you gave me—your wisdom, your guidance, your example, and your sharing. Thank you for bringing me up in the fear and reverence of God and to always put my trust in him.

Good-bye, farewell, and I will see you in the hereafter.

Many times you said, "A man's life writes his history." Your life leaves all of us a blessed history to pattern our lives after.

I love you, Dad, and you will always be a part of my life. Thank you for being the father you were.

Your son,

Ameal

Our First Home

There is nothing like providing a home of your own for your family. It fosters a sense of pride and the feeling that you have achieved a piece of the American dream. One of the first things we did—Henrietta and I—after I was hired by the US Postal Service was to start looking for a home to buy.

Barnett Grier, a Black realtor in the city and someone we knew and trusted, showed us houses out in the Sunny Slope area of Rubidoux. I don't know how many houses were in that subdivision at the time, but we looked at almost all of them and decided it was not where we wanted to live. We also looked at houses in La Sierra. At this time in the city's history, people of color were not welcomed into the community. One realtor, while showing us a house in La Sierra, talked about a ghost that appeared periodically in the home.

Finally, Barnett showed us a house on Norman Way—off Hillside Avenue—that we purchased for $10,500. Can you imagine today purchasing a three-bedroom home for $10,500? You cannot get a good used car for that price. But it's all relative. I was only making $2.18 an hour at the time.

I was a proud man when we moved into our new home. Every day after coming home from work, I spent time in the front yard planting flowers. I would like to think that my front yard was the most attractive on the street. The backyard was more of a challenge. It was uneven with trenches. It took a while, but I eventually smoothed it out and planted grass. I was proud of the improvement.

My next project was to repair the backyard fence. My backyard fence was adjoined by a home owner on Hillside Avenue whose last name was Hathaway—he was a professional musician. We split the cost and repaired the fence weaving white slats into the mesh-wire fence. Wow! It turned out much better than we anticipated.

Grandchildren

My father Stephen died in August, 1989. He was ninety-four years old. My first grandson—Stephen Ameal—was born a few days before his death. I have always thought God replaced Dad, whom I loved dearly, with my grandson Stephen Ameal. I enjoyed being present at his birth and taking him places and doing things with him as he grew up.

As we drove in the car, I would sing songs to amuse him. One song we sang often together was "Old MacDonald Had a Farm." I think Stephen really liked that song, and we both sang it with great enthusiasm. A few minutes after singing it, I would look over at him and find him sound asleep.

Shortly after the mall in Moreno Valley opened, I took Stephen to the carousel on the second floor. He was three years old and had a great time riding everything a little three-year-old could ride—mostly the carousel ponies. We must have spent an hour or so at the carousel, but when I was ready to go, little Stephen was not, and we had what I would call a standoff. Little Stephen stood right outside the entrance to the carousel, arms folded, lips poked out, and refused to leave. I took a seat in the food court, across from the carousel, and waited him out. He did not cry; he just made it very clear he was not ready to go. Finally, he gave in; I bought him a treat and took him home.

I think Stephen is musically inclined; at an early age he learned to play the saxophone. In fact, he played the sax at my seventieth birthday celebration at the home of my friends Chuck and Sally Beaty. With proper motivation and encouragement, he will do well in the field of music—on the technology side if not instrumentally.

Date with Granddaughter

In January 2003, I had a memorable time with my granddaughter, Lindsay. We attended the Black Police Banquet at the Hilton Hotel in Ontario, California, and I took Lindsay along as my date—she was eleven years old at the time. I was decked out in a tuxedo, and Lindsay was beautifully attired in a skirt and blouse.

Captain Jim Cannon of the Riverside Police Department was in charge of the program, and Leo Stallworth, a Black news reporter for NBC, was the guest speaker. Mr. Stallworth brought his nine—or ten-year-old daughter with him, and I ended up girl-sitting her and Lindsay. We had a delicious meal together, and I joined in the conversation between the two girls. What they talked about I do not remember, but it was typical talk for girls their age.

Prior to the meal, I was moving about from table to table, the girls with me, greeting the officers and guests. After dinner, the girls had to go to the restroom, so I had to chaperon them there and wait for them to come out. Leo Stallworth must have considered Lindsay and I godsends because we gave him the ability to greet the guests and to concentrate on his speech without worrying about his daughter; she was in good hands.

Lindsay has sight impairment, but it does not prevent her from achieving. In fact, she is a straight-A student. I expect great things from Lindsay because she enjoys learning. Whatever her dream is, I predict she will achieve it. If she has more than one dream, she will achieve them all.

Nkosi and Julian: Youngest Grandsons

Nkosi and Julian, my two youngest grandkids, are both very bright. They both have the ability to achieve their dream(s) and do great things in life.

Very early in Nkosi's childhood, his mother—Tyanne—taught him to read. We would be in the car riding someplace and she would teach him to read signs along the road. She taught him how to sound out the letters whenever he would have difficulty pronouncing a word. This went on all the time—whether they were in a car, airplane, or at home. It was fun and exciting to watch Tyanne teach Nkosi how to read.

Nkosi's parents enrolled him in a private school at a very early age and excelled in learning so that, at age eleven, he is a grade ahead of other kids his age. He seems to enjoy learning and has developed good study habits.

I played a significant role in teaching Nkosi to ride a bicycle. It was not easy. His mother Tyanne would watch us, and whenever Nkosi fell, she would rush to him, and he would start screaming. It took a while, but after a few bumps and bruises, he mastered the art of riding a bicycle.

Nkosi travels with his mother Tyanne everywhere she goes. T—as we call her—works for Alaska Airlines and is able to get passes on most airlines. Nkosi has logged more airline miles in his eleven years than I have in my entire life, and I have done a good bit of traveling myself.

It's fun to watch Nkosi and T scurry to and through the airport—Nkosi with a backpack pulling a small suitcase, and T nudging him along while pulling her own luggage. The airline stewards seem to delight in engaging Nkosi in conversation. Nkosi does not appear to be at all shy with them.

Nkosi should do well in any field of study he chooses. I believe he will be highly motivated because both his parents—Tyanne and Jeffery—will set the bar high for him, and he will not want to disappoint them. As I said earlier, Nkosi is very bright, and he is programmed to succeed. The foundation has been laid, and it is solid.

Julian Angel Moore

Julian Angel Moore, my youngest grandson, is a delightful child. He came late in the lives of my son Derwin Stephen (Steve) Moore and his wife Patricia. Their two older kids are Lindsay Charee and Stephen Ameal.

When Patricia told Lindsay that she was going to have a baby, Lindsay was very sad at first, until she found out it was going to be a boy. She seemed to be okay once she realized her position in the family was secure: she would be the only girl.

Julian has always been special to me. We bonded early and rode horses on broom sticks throughout the house; and of course we sang "Old MacDonald Had a Farm" together. He loved the "Ee i ee i oh" part, which I would really stress. I was also, from time to time, the horse that he rode.

I also taught Julian to ride the bicycle we bought him. He fell several times during the learning process, but he never cried; he would get back on the bike, and we would go at it again.

When Julian was old enough, I delighted in picking him up and taking him to Sunday school with me. He liked Sunday school—the nursery initially—and interacting with kids his age. One Sunday, when he was five or six years old, he asked if he could join the church and get baptized. Nothing could have pleased my wife Henrietta and me more. You see, Lindsay and Stephen had, years earlier, asked permission to join our old church—Second Baptist—and we did not give it, to our regret. With Julian, we seized the opportunity to redeem ourselves.

Julian and I had some interesting conversations on our way to and from Sunday school. They were not baby conversations. I would describe them as "a child's view of an evolving world" encountering my experience of "a world lived in seventy-plus years." He would tell me what he had learned in school and some things he liked to do, such as playing baseball. He told me his teacher's name and his favorite subject: math.

On the way home from Sunday school, I would take him to Rite Aid and treat him to his favorite ice cream, which varied from week to week. Additionally, he would con me into buying a miniature car as well as the ice cream—I enjoyed doing it.

I will always remember what happened to me after Sunday school one Sunday. I had planned to stay for the service but was feeling faint and light-headed, so I decided to take Julian home. The light-headed, faint feeling was getting worse. By the time I got Julian, I was really in bad shape—I knew I was going to pass out. I gave him my books to carry for me and on our way to the car, I sat down on a ledge alongside the church, and the next thing I knew, I opened my eyes from where I lay on the sidewalk. I saw people standing around me, and little Julian was holding my books and coat. Some lady, whom no one knew, had revived me with CPR, and the Fire Department and the ambulance had arrived to dispatch me to the emergency room at Kaiser Hospital.

At the hospital, I became concerned about how this incident might affect little Julian emotionally. When his parents brought him in to see me, I assured him that Grandpa was okay and that he was not to worry.

In retrospect, when people describe Julian's behavior surrounding this incident, I am really overwhelmed emotionally. He stood by his grandpa and stayed with me through it all. Thanks, Jule.

There is no doubt in my mind that Julian will excel at whatever he chooses to do in life. He will make a positive contribution to society and make his family proud.

"Train up a child in the way you would have him go, and when he is old, he will not depart from it."(theBible)

Below is a speech I gave to a group at Park Avenue Baptist Church commemorating Dr. Martin Luther King Jr.'s birthday in January 1999:

We are here tonight celebrating the birthday anniversary of Dr. Martin Luther King Jr. We celebrate his birthday anniversary because of his leadership, his vision, and the inspiration he provided us: his people. He was a Moses to his people. He said to Governor Wallace and Bull Connors, "let my people go" and took action to see that it happened.

If you are going to keep people in servitude, you must make them appear to be less than human. To justify slavery, we were declared to be more like animals than humans—savages. We were said to be lazy, stupid, the scum of the human race. We were despised and forever relegated to be the "hewers of wood and the drawers of water," and all too many of our people internalized this garbage.

The *declaration of inferiority* was reinforced by segregation laws: separate accommodations, separate drinking fountains, etc. They were supposed to be "separate but equal." However, nothing could have been further from the truth. In fact the reverse was true: they were *separate and totally unequal.*

To maintain the status quo, we were denied the right to vote, thereby denying us input concerning the laws that governed us, and we were declared by our adversaries to be *"happy."*

This was the society that I experienced growing up in the backwoods of Polarville, Mississippi, and it was the society that existed when Dr. King launched his nonviolent civil rights movement.

The son of a Baptist minister and a brilliant student, by the tender age of twenty-eight, Dr. King had obtained a PhD. He was eminently prepared to lead his people. He was in the right place at the right time. He was the Pastor of Dexter Avenue Baptist Church in Montgomery, Alabama, a stone's throw from the State Capitol when Rosa Park refused to give up her seat and move to the back of the bus as ordered. Never mind that Negroes, or Coloreds as we were then called (more accurately: Niggers or for those who were more sympathetic, Negras), paid the same fare as everyone else. But this incident gave birth to the civil rights movement with Dr. King as its leader.

Dr. King articulated who we were. He reminded us and the nation that we are human beings; that we are not cattle; that this country was built on the sweat, blood, and tears of our ancestors. When you build a house, you certainly are entitled to live in it and enjoy the fruits of your labor; we are native sons.

Dr. King made us realize that there are some things in life worth dying for. He said that life is not worth living unless there is something you are willing to die for. Liberty, freedom, and human dignity certainly are values worth the sacrifice. Without these God-given values, you are not living anyway; you just exist. Patrick Henry said, "Give me Liberty or give me death." Frederick Douglass, a slave that overpowered his slave master and obtained his freedom, stated: "When a slave can no longer be flogged, he is more than half free; power concedes nothing without a struggle."

Dr. King inspired our people to face vicious dogs, to face water hoses, bully clubs, lynch mobs, all while singing "We Shall Overcome." He made us understand that the cause for which we were marching, being abused, and going to jail was a just cause and worth the sacrifice. Because we made the sacrifice, the walls of segregation came tumbling down. However, the hatred for Dr. King was so intense that he paid the ultimate sacrifice—he was assassinated. But the things for which we struggled came to pass for the most part: the Civil Rights Act; the Voters Rights Act; public accommodations were open to all of us; school integration, and more.

Now we live in the *best of times* and the *worst of times* for our people. When we consider the best of times, we observe that we have more elected officials than ever before; more doctors and lawyers than ever before; more educators, writers, performers, college students, athletes, and more officers in the military. We have a growing middle class and command a lot of wealth and buying power. "We have moved on up to the east side and finally got a piece of the pie." (This is a line from a television program).

The worst of times are that in so doing we have abandoned our less fortunate brothers and sisters to the ghettos of the inner city. They are without jobs, without job skills. Their children attend schools that don't educate. Their children, for the most part, live in single-family households without father figures. They have no positive role models and are essentially raising themselves. They are joining gangs seeking acceptance; selling and using illegal drugs and filling the nation's prisons. Some of our best specimens are behind bars, and for those that serve their time and return to society, they are disenfranchised, unable to vote, cannot find work, and so they do what they did before and return to prison. There is a war going on among gangs and drug dealers, and our children are the victims.

We must remember that if we are going to get our children up the down escalator, they have to work harder, study harder, challenge themselves, and stretch themselves. We parents are the watch dogs and are responsible for getting our kids up the down escalator—let's make them run.

Second Baptist Church

We arrived in the city of Riverside in July 1960 and three months later (October), we joined Second Baptist Church. Second Baptist was in its final stage of construction; the main sanctuary was not complete, and Sunday services were held upstairs in what would become the dining/Sunday school assembly area.

Reverend William Thomas was the pastor. He was a warm, kind, loving Christian leader. To me, he was a father figure as I was only twenty-six years old at the time, and he reminded me of my father, with his strong Christian belief. He set the example for the membership, as he very closely lived the messages he preached.

Shortly after joining Second Baptist, I became a member of the choir. Ms. Luvenia Nash-Freeze was the director/ pianist and one of the best. She was better known as Luvenia Nash—founder and director of the Nash singers—an all-Negro choral group which has appeared many times in the Hollywood Bowl, Los Angeles Philharmonic Auditorium, Redlands Bowl, and Ramona Bowl and, through the years, in numerous films (information from Black Voice News). She was an accomplished individual well-known in the field of music. Most of us in the choir could not read notes; she taught us how to sight-read (to locate the note on the scale), and we were able to sing all the types of Christian music: the "Christmas Cantata," the "Hallelujah Chorus," "The Messiah," etc. Pastor Thomas helped to motivate and encourage the choir by frequently saying to us, "I have traveled all over the world, but when I want to hear some beautiful singing I come back home to Second Baptist, down by the riverside."

During the time I was a member at Second Baptist—1960-2003—I had the honor of serving in every church office except the board of deacons; I felt unworthy to serve in such a position.

But getting back to the choir, I really enjoyed singing in the choir and looked forward to rehearsals. Most of us in the choir were in our late twenties or early thirties and therefore were energetic, enthusiastic, and, at times show-offs. There was one older member of the choir—Sister Emma Lou James—who would always remind us just before the closing prayer to "be loving and kind toward each other." She did this at every choir rehearsal she attended, and we tried to conform to her advice.

By the way, Sister Emma Lou James and Sister Rosa Jones—both members of the choir—were very good friends and often traveled to different events together. Sister James owned a very nice automobile and of course did the driving, but Sister Jones was the controller, meaning that she tried to control Sister James's speed. She drove like a bat out of Hades, so Sister Jones was a busy controller.

One member of the choir—B. J. Johnson—stuttered but had a beautiful, deep bass voice and used it very effectively. He was a strong, faithful Christian, a deacon, and he put his soul into his singing and all his church endeavors. The choir was so fond of him that when he died at an early age, the choir named a singing group "The B. J. Johnson Singers" in his honor.

Another very interesting individual in the choir was Skidmore Granderson. Skidmore had difficulty staying on key—if he was ever on key in the first place—but he was faithful. He attended almost every rehearsal and participated in most of the choir's programs. He sang just low enough so that only a few people in the choir heard him—those standing next to him and maybe one or two others. Grandy, as we affectionately called him, had a good sense of humor; therefore it did not bother him when a member of the choir said to him, "Grandy, you couldn't carry a tune in a bucket." Even the choir director appreciated Grandy's faithfulness. After working unsuccessfully to get him to sing in tune, she praised him for his attendance.

Two men that touched my heart when they sang solo or together were L. C. Goins and Robert (Bob) Hasson. Bob in particular has a beautiful singing voice to this day; it's probably better now than it was back then. Two women in the choir that fell into the same category as L. C. and Bob were Francis Aaron and Leona Coleman. On special occasions they sang duets together that were very touching. I was always touched by the song "Give Me My Flowers," which they sang on special occasions. In other words, the song lyrics essentially say, don't wait until I am dead to give me flowers. Give them to me while I can still smell them and appreciate them.

Some years later, I had the honor and the privilege of serving as the president of the choir. I remember back in the 1970s, the choir sponsored a musical program titled: "Negro Music Past and Present." Ms. Nash, the choir director, teamed up with Clarence Muse, a motion picture actor, in putting the program together. They both lived out in the West Perris community in close proximity to each other. Clarence Muse's property was known as Muse Awhile Ranch. We had several rehearsals for the program at the Muse Awhile Ranch. We had fun before and after rehearsals, but the actual rehearsals were serious business. The program turned out to be very successful and attracted a large attendance at Second Baptist Church.

Sunday School

Another auxiliary of the church I enjoyed was Sunday school. Sunday school provides the opportunity to learn more about God's word, and you can question and have a dialogue with the teacher/instructor. I can't jump up in the middle of church service and ask a question about what the preacher is saying. Besides, I was raised at a very early age in the Sunday school, and when I was in high school, I served as the secretary until I graduated and went into the air force. Therefore, Sunday school is my favorite church auxiliary.

It seemed like Brother John Travis, the Sunday school superintendent at New Welcome Baptist Church, opened the Sunday school with the song "Shine on Me" 90 percent of the time. It would have been nice after a hard week's work in the hot sun to open with "Showers of Blessings" to cool me off.

I wanted my sons—Henrietta and I had three sons—to have a similar experience; I therefore took them to Sunday school and church every Sunday. I would reward them by stopping at the Tasty Freeze on the way home and let them order what they wanted; years, I would serve more than four years as the Sunday school superintendent of Second Baptist Church.

Every year during my tenure, I attended the National Baptist Sunday School Convention. I learned a lot, enjoyed the experience, and implemented many of the ideas presented at the convention.

Board of Trustees

I had the privilege of serving on the church board of trustees for several years—one or two years as its chairman. During my tenure, we implemented the practice of depositing church funds collected immediately after counting. Before this practice was put in place, the funds were locked in the safe at Second Baptist, and Brother George Sanders—the custodian—made the deposit sometime during the week, usually on Monday. But there were a few trustees that complained about the inaccuracy of the deposit, and that is why I changed the method of depositing the funds.

Brother Sanders was totally dedicated to Second Baptist Church; he loved the church. Brother Sanders fixed whatever it was that needed to be fixed, often paying for the parts out of his own funds. But, as usual, there were those that said he was not earning the small stipend he was paid. For whatever reason, Brother Sanders took a leave of absence from his custodial duties, and it took three people to replace him. Needless to say, that was the end of the complaints against Brother Sanders.

Reverend Thomas was the pastor of Second Baptist Church for sixty-three years. There was no assistant pastor. Reverend

Will Edmond served as the assistant to the pastor but not as Assistant Pastor. Reverend Edmond took charge of church services once each year, when Pastor Thomas went on vacation. However, Reverend Edmond played a very effective role in the church. He regularly visited the sick and shut-ins at their homes or in the hospital. He was also extremely dedicated to Pastor Thomas and became his eyes and ears when the pastor lost his eyesight. He accompanied Reverend Thomas everywhere he went and saw that all his needs were fulfilled.

It's too bad that Pastor Thomas did not groom him as his replacement—he did not groom a replacement, period. Reverend Edmond did, however, serve as the interim pastor while the church looked for a replacement following Pastor Thomas's death. Reverend Munford served briefly as pastor, followed by Reverend T. Ellsworth Gantt, the current pastor. Today Pastor Thomas would not recognize the church he built, loved, and cherished. Most of the members under Reverend Thomas's leadership are no longer there, and the church as he knew it no longer exists.

Another interesting member of Second Baptist Church was Reverend R. R. Montgomery. Reverend Montgomery got to preach maybe once a year. He was very practical and used visual aids to assist in getting his message across to the audience. He would line his visuals up in front of the pulpit before delivering his message and would point to them as the message unfolded; whether you understood the message or not, he held your attention.

Reverend Montgomery also sold Watkins products: ointment, lotion, liniment, etc. In case you are not familiar with Watkins products, whatever your needs were, Watkins had a product for it. Individuals sold them door-to-door—it was somewhat like Avon but without the house parties.

Years later, when I was superintendent of support services at the post office on Chicago Avenue, Reverend Montgomery would drop by with a request for a loan of a few dollars. I would advance him five to ten dollars without expecting to be repaid, and usually I was not. In any event, I loved Reverend Montgomery; he had a good Christian spirit.

MLK Statue

During the 1990s (1993), I was part of the MLK monument visionaries, a community group. Our goal was to erect a statue of Dr. Martin Luther King Jr. somewhere in the downtown area. Some of the other committee members were: Alan and Jan Pauw, PhDs; Lulamae Clemons, PhD; Rose Mayes (Chairman); Reverend and Ms Johnny Harris; Rose Oliver, and others whose names eludes me. I hope they will forgive me.

To cover the cost of the statue, our goal was to raise $150 thousand dollars. We started out soliciting small contributions at fund-raisers. Years passed, but we were nowhere near our goal. In fact I had been elected to the city council when the committee met at the home of Chuck and Sally Beaty—Chuck, as I've mentioned earlier, was also a member of city council—to discuss the situation and come up with an action plan. I think we had a couple of meetings at the Beaty's home before deciding to solicit pledges of a thousand dollars toward the statue, realizing it would take us ten to fifteen years to fund the project at our current rate.

The young lady that designed and produced the statue was a strong supporter of the civil rights movement. She produced a statue unique to any I have seen of Dr. Martin Luther King Jr. She depicted him walking with his hands on the shoulders of two young children; he is walking with them in a flowing robe that embodies the major highlights of the civil rights movement. In fact, I would say the movement's entire history is captured on the robe.

After we had come up with a method to raise the funds for the statue, Toni Kachevas—an employee at city hall—worked with us to identify a site for the statue. She also scheduled our visits to a plant nursery in Brea to select trees to surround the statue. Toni turned out to be invaluable in cutting the red tape and getting things done. I don't know what we would have done without her—it certainly would have taken a lot longer to complete the project. We selected magnolia trees to surround the statue, as we thought they were closely identified with the South.

After the statue was erected, we held a dedication and unveiling ceremony. Yolanda King, Dr. King's eldest daughter, traveled from Los Angeles in order to participate. Yolanda was a movie actress who lived in Los Angeles at the time of the ceremony. Yolanda said the statue was the most compelling one she had seen of her father.

My colleague and good friend Chuck Beaty could not attend the ceremony, as he was recuperating from the three gunshot wounds he received at city hall on October 6, 1998. His wife, and our good friend Sally Beaty, was his representative, and it turned out to be a joyous occasion for all in attendance. Currently, there are several statues on the Main Street Mall downtown, but in significance, I believe the MLK statue outshines them all.

One committee member whom I respect and admire—Alan Pauw, PhD—has always been involved in worthwhile causes in the city and was very supportive of minorities. Alan, for example, was a cofounder of Saturday Morning Toastmasters. The idea was to use toastmasters' techniques and training to help prepare minorities for leadership positions. Additionally, Alan would always invite minorities to functions in which his accounting firm had purchased a table. Personally, Alan got me involved in several organizations in the city: the Parliamentary Procedure Club, the Astronomical Society, Rotary International, and I was also a cofounder of Saturday Morning Toastmasters.

There's an interesting story behind how I stopped saying "Dr. Pauw" and began calling him "Alan." During the time that we interacted with each other, our friendship grew. So, following some function we had attended together, Dr. Pauw called me aside and said to me, "Ameal, my friends call me Alan." From that day forward I called him Alan because he was my friend.

Both Alan and his wife Jan—Jan was a linguist and spoke seven different languages—are now deceased, but they were both solid as the rock of Gibraltar. I learned a lot from them both. They lived lives and set examples worth following.

Gala in the Desert

Chancellor Ray (Raymond) Orbach came to UCR in 1995 from UCLA. He immediately set a goal to grow the University to twenty-five thousand students—the enrollment at the time was between eight and ten thousand. He also wanted to establish a medical school and move the athletic program to Division I, just to mention a few of his goals.

UCR and the City of Riverside scheduled monthly meeting during Chancellor Orbach's administration to ensure good communication. Chuck Beaty and I were the council representatives at the monthly meetings, along with Mayor Ron Loveridge.

During those meetings, we often discussed University Village, which was a joint project between the city's Redevelopment Department and UCR. The Village not only provided activities for the students and the public—movies, restaurants, video games, Starbucks, etc—but classes were also held in the theaters there.

A program implemented By UCR called The Gala in the Desert was attended by the city and UCR. The purpose was to raise funds for UCR by way of featuring dignitaries as speakers. If my memory serves me correctly, Chuck and I attended all the galas. The first gala featured General Colin Powell, a hero of mine. To me, General Powell was larger than life, especially so after I read his book, *My American Journey*. I believe that General Powell could have been elected president of the USA, if he had chosen to run for the office. Anyway, to meet him in person, shake his hand, and have my picture taken with him—along with Chuck and councilwoman Maureen Kane—was an experience I shall never forget.

At the first gala the ones that followed, I had the pleasure and the privilege of meeting former president Gerald Ford. I have yet to meet a more gracious and humble man. President L. B. Johnson had painted a mental picture of him as someone who had played too much football without a helmet; in other words, that he was not very bright. Once you met President Ford, you realized this assessment was inaccurate and strictly politics.

Every year the city council received an invitation from UCR to attend the Gala in the Desert. Chuck, Maureen, and I, to my remembrance, were the only council members to attend. In addition to General Colin Powell, other featured guests were: Prime Minister Tony Blair of Great Britain as well as a female prime minister, but I do not remember what country she was from or her name. Each year I looked forward to the Gala in The Desert and was disappointed when the program ended. Many thanks to Michael Beck and Robert Nava, who coordinated this program out of the office of Vice Chancellor Jim Erickson. And a big thanks to you, Jim Erickson.

America's Promise Alliance

In 1997, I was part of a delegation from the City of Riverside and UCR that traveled to Philadelphia, Pennsylvania to witness the kickoff of America's Promise. General Colin Powell was its founding chairman. The delegation consisted of Chancellor Ray Orbach, selected staff members and students at UCR, and representatives of the City of Riverside.

The idea of America's Promise grew out of the Presidents' Summit for America's Future in 1997. Every living president was present except for Reagan, but his wife Nancy represented him.

The day began by watching the Secret Service and the Philadelphia police escort the presidents into the city. I believe they were taken to a park in a lower-income neighborhood. Ed Rendell was the mayor of Philadelphia at the time, and he would later become the Governor of Pennsylvania.

Approximately thirty governors, a hundred mayors, one hundred forty-five community delegations, and prominent business leaders attended the summit. The program was sponsored by the Points of Light Foundation, the Corporation for National and Community Service, and United Way of America. We made five promises to help our youth succeed:

- Caring adults
- Safe places,
- A healthy start
- Effective education
- Opportunity to help others

That night, Oprah Winfrey presided as master of ceremonies of a concert at city hall. There were lots of performers on the program, but the one I remember, one of my favorite among singers, was Tony Bennett. Of course Tony sang his signature song, "I Left My Heart in San Francisco," and I do not remember much after that.

The program continued the next day in an area adjacent to the hotel where our delegation was lodged. Once again, Oprah served as master of ceremonies and brought energy and excitement to the activities. I did not get to shake her hand, but I will always remember her as the master of ceremony of the program: Memories Light the Corners of My Mind.

My Run for Mayor

A sea change took place following the police department's killing of Tyisha Miller. The state attorney general, Bill Lockyer, applied sanctions/stipulated judgements to the police department—mostly pertaining to training and operation of the Riverside Police Department. An individual was appointed by the Attorney General to monitor the Riverside Police Department to see that the sanctions were adhered to, the cost of which was paid for by Riverside's police department. Police Chief Jerry Carroll—a good, courageous man—lost his job for doing the right thing. He fired the four officers involved in killing Tyisha Miller. Stan Yamamoto, the city attorney, resigned under pressure, and so did city manager John Holmes. All of these individuals were good people determined to do what they felt was the right thing about the shooting. As I said earlier, I particularly appreciated Chief Carroll's courage and his decision to fire the four officers involved in the killing of Tyisha Miller.

George Caravahlo, the city manager of Santa Clarita, became Riverside's new city manager. The council and the mayor interviewed several candidates and unanimously selected George Caravahlo. I really liked a Black city managerin

Reno, Nevada, but he appeared to have some reservations about leaving his position in Reno. George Caravahlo came prepared, impressed us with his presentation, and was unanimously selected.

When George arrived in Riverside, he began by meeting with various groups to get a feel for what goals and priorities should be set for the city. This process culminated in a meeting at the Convention Center here in Riverside, open to all that wanted to give input. It was a great turnout and very successful in gathering input from the citizens, and George set the city's goals and priorities based on these meetings. But there were a few council members who were upset because George did not get council's approval before scheduling the meeting.

Later, when George began to staff his administration and request resources to put his plans into action—plans based on the priorities and goals set by the citizens—the majority of the council and the mayor did not support him. My position concerning the matter was, "Give him what he wants/needs, and hold him accountable if he doesn't produce." The mayor, who I thought at first was supportive of the new city manager, evidently felt left out and withdrew his support.

Now, I have always been a strong supporter of Mayor Ron Loveridge. I was president of the local chapter of the NAACP when he first ran for the First Ward council seat, and was an admirer and supporter up to this time. In fairness to Ron, he appointed me to Boards and Commissions that set the stage for my later city council run. I served with some of the movers and shakers of the city: lawyers, judges, administrators, etc. I think Mayor Loveridge was/is a good mayor but the city manager, according to the city charter, is responsible for running the city. The position of mayor is more of a ceremonial position. The mayor can influence the direction of the city—articulate its priorities and goals—but the real power belongs to the city manager. The city charter clearly spells out the duties and responsibilities of the council, city manager, and mayor.

George never got the resources he wanted. His adversaries did not give way, and he was forced to resign. George was the first minority city manager in Riverside (as far as I am aware), and I sometimes wondered if this had anything to do with the council's unwillingness to work with him. Now, I am an eternal optimist; I see the glass as half-full instead of half-empty, but it upset me to witness his treatment. After the selection of the next city manager, I grew even more curious about George's treatment.

George was replaced by Brad Hudson from the county's EDA(Environmental Department Agency). He was approved by the Search Committee on the recommendation of First Ward councilman Dom Betro, who knew him. I was serving as mayor pro tem at the time and, with the help of Third Ward councilman Art Gage, negotiated Brad's initial salary as city manager. Brad Hudson's treatment following his appointment was a 180 degree shift from the council's treatment of George Caravahlo. Brad got anything he so much as *thought* he wanted, seemly without any opposition. This heightens my suspicion concerning George's treatment. Do not misunderstand me; I like Brad Hudson. I voted for him and approved his requests for staffing and resources. I also think he has been an effective city manager—he got things done. But the council's very different reactions to George and Brad prompted me to run for mayor.

It was 2005, the last year of my third term as Second Ward councilman. I was up for reelection in November, but I had already decided not to run for a fourth term. When I informed my close friends Chuck and Sally Beaty, they encouraged me to run for mayor. It really didn't take much encouragement, as I had already given it some thought to use my candidacy as a way to protest the treatment of George Caravahlo and to articulate how I thought the city of Riverside could improve.

To see what kind of support I might have, Chuck and I had lunch in the Canyon Crest Shopping Center with Nick Tavaglione and Richard Ramirez; everything considered, the meeting went well.

Not too long after the meeting in Canyon Crest, I filed my candidacy for mayor, paid the filing fee, and collected the required number of registered voters' signatures in support. The next thing I needed to do was put together a campaign committee.

My campaign committee consisted of the following individuals: Nick Tavaglione, Rich Ramirez, Henry Coil, Del Roberts, Roger Castro, Chuck Beaty, Dorothy Bailey, George Caravalho, Tim and Cynthia Desoto, Toni Kachevas, Jalani Bakari, Carl Moore, Rich Stalder, Katie Wider, and Lindsay Abercrombie. I appointed Cynthia Desoto to the role of campaign chairperson—she was one of the best.

We held our first few meetings at Nick Tavaglione's home. Here we identified the issues the campaign should address and the issues we thought people were most interested in. Subsequently, we moved into an office in the Canyon Crest Town Center provided by Mark Thompson, the center's owner. Sally Beaty decorated the office with my plaques, awards, and certificates. We were ready to begin.

The campaign kickoff took place on April 18, 2005 at the Romano Restaurant in Canyon Crest Town Center. Following is the speech I gave to the audience:

> Good evening and welcome. I want to thank you for being here tonight. Your support for my candidacy as mayor is very important to me.

> My wife Henrietta and I came to Riverside in 1960 when I was a staff sergeant in the air force. We were fascinated by the palm trees, the orange groves, the fragrance of the orange blossoms, and the beautiful snowcapped mountains that paint such a lovely picture in the winter. We decided to make Riverside our home

> I was fortunate to establish a rewarding career with the US Postal Service, but serving my community was equally important to me. I wanted to make a difference. I became involved in various community organizations, such as the NAACP, United Way, Urban League, and North High School's first

Site Council, to name a few. I served seven years on the Parking, Traffic, and Streets Commission and seven years on the Planning Commission. In January 1994, I was elected to the city council. My opponent was a former mayor. I am currently serving in my twelfth year on the council.

The duties and responsibilities of the council members, the city manager, and the Mayor are clearly spelled out in the city charter. To move this city forward, I will work with the elected officials, the new city manager, and staff to come together as a team, while at the same time respecting each person's assigned role and set of responsibilities in accordance with the charter.

In sports, teams that win championships are those in which each member effectively executes his or her assigned roles. Their goal is to win, not concern themselves about who will be the most valuable player. As your mayor, I will help unite this city, and we will move it forward together. I will not concern myself about who gets the credit. I see myself as a team builder; a voice of reason. With my background and diverse experiences, I am ready to become your mayor. I vow to bring fresh energy, vision, and leadership to the office. It is time to get back to the basics of good government. Clear and consistent support of the city charter by the mayor and council will allow the city manager and staff to better serve the residents or Riverside. We must lead by example.

Join me and let each of us play our role to make Riverside the best city in the state of California. I promise you, when I am elected, there will be "Moore for everyone." Thank you again for your ongoing support.

The committee met once a week, but as the candidate, I visited the office daily. Our campaign manager, Cynthia Desoto, scheduled meetings with different groups, and we walked precincts, knocked on doors, and talked to a lot of people. We lost the election, but my only disappointment was in the small number of votes I received. Sometimes, you just want to get a message across to the people, and that I did.

One campaign committee member that I particularly came to admire and respect was developer Henry Coil; Henry not only attended every committee meeting, he also supported the campaign generously with his funds. I really praised Henry to my family and friends. I told them not to be offended when Henry refers to Blacks as "Colored folks," and that he was a sincere, genuine, loveable individual. I include Henry Coil as a reliable friend I can trust. You are a good man, Henry. Thank you very much for being my friend and supporter.

When Henrietta and I arrived in Riverside in 1960, the population was about sixty thousand people. In 2011, it is well over three hundred thousand. The city is five times larger than what it was in 1960, and one can live wherever one can afford a home. In 1960, the Black population was mostly housed on the east side of Riverside with a spattering in Casa Blanca, and areas off Hillside Street were beginning to open up to them. In other words, Riverside was basically a segregated city. There were still covenants in housing contracts against sales to Black people. In fact, when I bought a home on Wroxton Drive in 1970, such was the situation—unenforceable though it was.

On Wroxton Drive, we lived next door to a deputy sheriff. I have yet to meet a more racist Caucasian, but his wife and children were very nice. In fact, his youngest son was between our oldest and middle son in age. When his dad was not home, he would climb over the fence and play basketball with my sons and their playmates. However, he kept his eyes on alert for his dad and would scurry back over the fence when he returned home. I observed this routine with amusement; how innocent kids are, how they can get along with each other if only adults would let them be kids. These were *teachable* opportunities for adults to encourage fair play, to encourage respect for each other, to encourage team spirit, to foster goodwill and friendship. I tried to do just that as I watched the kids play basketball together in my backyard.

What happens to children during their formative years can stay with them in adulthood—good or bad. One such situation has stayed in the mind of my oldest son Jeff to this day. He was in ninth grade at Ramona High School and was riding his bike home from band practice. He cut through the parking lot at Sears about the time they were closing the auto shop. Someone slammed the garage door closed, which made a loud noise. The police happened to drive by about the same time and stopped my son Jeff and accused him of throwing a rock at the building. Of course Jeff denied any such thing and asked if he could call home to his parents, as he was afraid that we would be concerned if he was not home soon; it was dark, and he was being intimidated by the police for no reason. The police finally let him go home, as there was no evidence that he had done anything wrong. Jeff never forgot this incident, and he views law enforcement with suspicion to this day.

I would hold up our neighbor the deputy sheriff as the perfect example of someone who should not be in law enforcement, as he was too biased. He had a superiority complex as far as Black people were concerned. Having a Black family live next door must have made him feel that he was regressing instead of progressing. We lived next door to him for seven years prior to moving to Celeste Drive. I imagine it was a great relief for him when we moved. But I had "promises to keep and miles go before I sleep." So I had to get going to help make Riverside a better place than I found it.

It must be miserable to live life disliking others based on their skin color. We all have one creator who wanted a beautiful flower garden of different colors, so he could have a lovely bouquet. We all have different attributes, different talents; these talents, when blended together, enrich the nation and the world. As we develop our talents and use them as we have been instructed by our creator to do, we help make the world a better place.

Mrs. Torres and Family

One family that I particularly came to admire and respect was the Torres family. I first met the Torres family in 1993 during my initial run for city council. Steven Torres was a candidate for city council along with Ab Brown, me, and one or two others. Steven had to be the youngest in the race and probably just met the minimum age requirement to run for the city council. His mother, Mrs. Torres, is the one that really got my attention. She was a single parent raising three children and was very involved in their lives and in the community. She was present at all the candidates' forums in support of her son.

Mrs. Torres is a strong individual and evidently set very high goals for her children—I am sure she was the one who encouraged her son Steven to run for city council. She is only about five feet tall physically but extremely strong in her beliefs and values. When I won the Second Ward council seat, she became one of my strongest supporters. I could count on the Torres family vote, and she persuaded her friends and acquaintances to support me as well. Mrs. Torres did whatever I asked her to do for me, and she seemed pleased that she was able to help. Of course, as her councilman I did whatever I could to improve the neighborhood in which she lived. Her son Steven got into some trouble at school, and the police pursued him. He disappeared from Riverside for a year or two but is now back and, according to Mrs. Torres, continuing his education.

I have been off the council since February, 2006, but Mrs. Torres and I remain friends, and she still asks me for advice on issues rather than her councilman. She is a sincere, reliable friend.

The youngest man to be elected to the council since I have been in Riverside was Eric Haley. Eric was elected to the city council shortly after graduating from UCR. If I recall correctly, Eric later ran unsuccessfully for mayor—he did, however, garner more votes than I had when I ran for Mayor in 2005. I befriended Eric and supported him in his run for elected office; when he later married and became a father, Henrietta and I babysat for him and his wife. I also had the pleasure of serving with him many years later when he was director of RCTC (Riverside County Transportation Commission) and I was a board member. I think Eric was an effective director and accomplished much during his term.

Steven Torres, if he had won the city council election in November, 1993 would have been the youngest person elected to that office. But if he had won, I would not have realized my dream of being elected and serving twelve years on the council—the most rewarding twelve years of my life. In any event, thanks you, Mrs. Torres, for being a friend and supporter.

Oneal's Widow and Children

Deputy Sheriff Oneal Moore would be proud of his family were he alive today. They all have done very well in their chosen careers and in their marriages. Oneal and his wife Mavella had four daughters: Veronica, Regina, Tresslar, and Sheronda. Oneal allegedly had a fifth daughter outside of marriage: Pam. In any event, all of my brothers—including me—are single-gender fathers for the most part. I am the father of three sons; Oneal was the father of four girls; Arthur, the father of four sons; Curtis, the father of one son; Caldwell, the father of two sons; and Ivory, the father of one girl. I'm not sure about my oldest brother, Pressie. I don't know the number of children in his family and their gender. I know he did have a son—Joseph (Joe) Moore—who he had evidently named after his great-granddad Joseph (Joe) Moore, who lived with Oneal and his wife Mavella for a while.

Mae (Mavella) is to be commended for the outstanding job she has done in raising her girls in a single-parent household. The family is very close and supportive of each other, and the girls have great love and respect for Mae. From the information I have, the family meets together somewhere at least once during the year. They all seem to put God first in their lives, and as a result they have all been blessed, and that includes Pam, who I know has strong faith in God. I love all of them very much, and it is very comforting to me to know they are all doing well—my heart smiles within me.

My Sons

I have always been proud to be a father. I feel blessed that the Lord entrusted me with three sons. I have tried to be a responsible parent; I tried to lay a strong foundation for them. They were raised in Sunday school and in church. Henrietta and I tried to involve them in wholesome recreation activities: Little League Baseball, the school's band. Although we didn't have much discretionary income when the boys were growing up, we went on a family vacation every year. My sons shared that their friends at school and in the neighborhood were jealous of these vacations. Well, that had not been my intention. We went on vacations to broaden their horizons; to immerse them in nature, so that they could appreciate the God-given natural beauty provided for us here on earth.

As they were growing up, we had clues to their later pursuits in life. For example, when taking the long drive back to Mississippi to visit our parents and relatives, Jeffery, the oldest, slept most of the way; Steve, the middle son, read the map for me; and Carl, our youngest son, spent the ride drawing. Today I would say that Jeff is the intellectual in the family; he reads a lot, likes to talk, and he graduated from the University of California, San Diego. Steve is adventuresome risk-taker. For the most part, he has been in business as an independent contractor. He has made a lot of money but, being a free spirit, spent it all and saved none. Steve is now on a new business adventure with a partner called eClose. It is a real estate appraisal business available nationwide. It has been incorporated, and shares into the business are being solicited. If Steve has learned anything from the past, he will be successful. He should have gained some wisdom from past experiences. Carl is artistic. He is in computer graphics. If you explain to Carl what it is you want, he will come up with a design. His shortcoming is his lack of self-confidence. Once he overcomes this lack of confidence, he is going to soar. I think he is well on his way to doing just that. In December, 2010, Carl left Riverside to pursue employment in San Antonio, Texas. He has not yet obtained the job he intended, but he is working and optimistic about his future. Living alone in a new environment can be a good thing—you have to depend on yourself and make new friends.

I believe Jeff would make an effective politician. His major in college was political science. He is a man of virtue, loyal; he is also concerned about the greater good of the community and the nation. These character traits are rare in individuals and embody a persuasive talent that is effective in getting legislation passed. His shortcoming is second-guessing himself. He has great ideas but slows to put them into action and will *think* his way out of them. Personally, I like to sleep on an idea; if I feel the same way the next morning, I go for it.

Jeff has strong feelings about racial issues. While he was a student at University of California, San Diego (UCSD), he sent the following poem to Henrietta and me as a Christmas gift. I think it gives insight into his feeling about race:

You're Just as Good

When he was young, his mama used to say,
"Son, don't let those folks treatcha that way,
It's like a shame that you stand out, but in your
Mind, there should be no doubt
You're just as good."

The words were strange, yet were ingrained
Very deep within him.
Father/son talks on long, long walks were filled
With words of wisdom,
But when those folks, in hate, would poke,
The words became a syndrome:
"You're just as good."

The boy now grown, is out on his own
To get an education.
Each test he takes, with fear he shakes
From grades that he's not makin.'

At night he hears, awakes with tears
From thoughts that are not ancient.
His questions of wise words called love
Come from a simple statement:

"You're just as good."

Now he has sought, through careful thought
The meaning of this phrase.
And soon it's clear; all is revealed,
The lifting of his haze:

You're just as good as those folks.
It has a double meaning.
The surface says you're a person,
A star that's truly gleaming, but in
Your heart there grows a poison
Called self-doubt.
No matter what you do or try, those
Folks, they show more clout.

Awareness overcame his deeply set thoughts of pain
With vows that he won't make a future,
Same mistake.

I hope that you have heard
The message in my words and see the revelation
That as I sing, to you I bring
Advice for a new nation:

Don't say it, don't say it.
The phrase, it has two meanings.
The more it's used to life their hearts,
The lower it will swing.

Jeff, you are just as good; in many aspects, you're even better. Keep your chin up and your head high. You can achieve anything in life you aspire to if you are willing to work hard and put God first.

When my sons were growing up, I enjoyed taking them to Dodgers baseball games. We would go to at least one home game each season. I was a dyed-in-the-wool Dodgers fan probably. This probably centered on Jackie Robinson breaking baseball's color barrier with the team. In any event, we really enjoyed those trips to Dodger Stadium. We always ended up in the left field pavilion—seemingly, that was where all the fun was. Besides, the seats were cheap and close to both the Dodgers' bullpen and the concession stand. My middle son, Steve, made many trips to the concession stand to get Dodger Dogs for himself and his brothers. Also, before the game started, the boys were able to get autographs from some of the outfielders. The difficult part for me was driving home after the game. My three sons would all fall asleep, and

I would have to fight sleep myself most of the way home. Those were fun times for my sons, and to this day, they still reminisce about their trips to Dodger Stadium—I, too, have fond memories of those trips.

Sisters: Vera and Elizabeth

Growing up, I had fun teasing my two younger sisters —Vera Mae and Elizabeth. Elizabeth was somewhat plump (Mom would call her "stout"), and Vera Mae was puny (small). There was a blacksmith in the community by the name of McCollum that worked out of a shed/garage at the home of the Richardson's (Ed and Bessie Richardson). I teased Elizabeth by calling her Bottle, Bottle, Bottle, and Vera Mae by calling her Puny Bone, Puny Bone, Puny Bone. They would call me McCollum, McCollum, McCollum; I guess I must have looked like Mr. Mc Collum whose looks was not that flattering. This would go on for an extended period of time until Elizabeth and Vera Mae grew upset with me and started crying. Then Mom would intervene and break it up.

Vera Mae did not like for Mom to comb her hair and would start crying the moment she saw Mom get the comb. I would begin teasing her, "Here it comes, it's getting cloudy, and there will be a rain storm in a few minutes." Vera would cry the whole time Mom was combing her hair. One thing I never understood; Dad used to comb her hair, and she never, to my knowledge, cried. Was it Dad's touch that made the difference?

Vera was a good student in school and went on to college at Alcorn A&M—an all-Black college at the time—and got her bachelor'sdegree. The last year at college, she was voted Miss Alcorn, and her future husband—Willie Bullock—was voted Mr. Alcorn. They were married shortly after graduation and had two sons together—Bruce and Eric. They made their home in Jackson, Mississippi, where Vera was a school teacher for thirty years and Willie worked for the Agriculture Department. He spent some time in Vietnam as well.

The marriage, unfortunately, did not last very long and Vera, for the most part, raised Bruce and Eric as a single parent. She did a good job keeping her sons involved in wholesome activities. As an example, both Bruce and Eric are Eagle Scouts. They both obtained college degrees and are gainfully employed. Bruce's degree is in business administration, and he currently works for the US Waterway. Eric's degree is in business administration with a minor in marketing from Mississippi State University in Starkville, Mississippi. He also has a masters of health services administration from Mississippi College in Clinton, Mississippi, which he obtained in May of 2010. He is currently employed at a Social Security Agency and is studying to get a PhD in social work.

As for Elizabeth, she was homecoming Queen in her last year of high school, and after graduation, she married Henry Lee Daniels. The consummation of this marriage produced two children, a boy and a girl: Rickey and Eskeletha. Shortly after the birth of Eskeletha, Henry Lee was involved in an accident in Galveston, Texas which left him paralyzed for the remainder of his life. Elizabeth had to take care of him as well as their two children until he died. Henry Lee was a stern, loving father from his wheelchair, and he and Elizabeth motivated Rickey and Eskeletha to go to college and obtain degrees. Rickey obtained his BS Degree in 1978 from Jackson State College in Jackson, Mississippi. Additionally, in 1978 he was commissioned as a second lieutenant after completing the Infantry Officer Basic Leadership Course in Fort Benning, Georgia; he obtained his MS degree in 1981 from Illinois Institute of Technology in Chicago, Illinois. Eskeletha obtained her degree from the University of Southern Mississippi, located in Hattiesburg, Mississippi.

Rickey met his wife, Uesky Phipps, at Jackson State University. She is from the Dominican Republic. They married after graduation and are the parents of three girls: Andrea, Bethany, and Chelsea. The oldest, Andrea, obtained her doctorate in psychology last year (2010); in fact she and her husband, Justin Anderson, both received doctorate degrees in Psychology in 2010.

Eskeletha married Tyrone Dorsey who became an officer in the air force and obtained the rank of major before retiring. They are the parents of twin girls: Karletha and Darletha.

Foundation: Mom and Dad

I am so very grateful to Mom and Dad for the grounding they gave me in childhood; as a result, I built my adult life on a solid foundation. The training, discipline, and the wisdom they provided guided and directed my life along my way in the world. Oh, I have strayed but, there has always been a hand pulling me back on the straight and narrow path and a still, soft voice telling me: "You were not raised like that; watch your behavior."

The entire village where I was nurtured did indeed raise the child. The same values taught in the home were reinforced at school and at church. The adults in the community also helped to modify youngsters' behavior. For the most part, all an adult had to say was, "I am going to tell your parents if you don't behave yourself."

Mom and Dad alerted their children to potential problems by statements such as, "I don't want you associating with so-and-so because he/she will get you in trouble" or, "Stay away from him; he is up to no good." Wow, what keen insight and wisdom. My parents could see and understand what I, at a tender age, could not. Obedience to their instructions kept us out of trouble and our family's good reputation intact. It takes years to build a good reputation, but it takes only one incident to tear it down. One thing we have to remember is that we as individuals are not the only ones affected by our actions—our loved ones are affected too, family and close friends. So we should try to be on our best behavior at all times.

Willie Brown

During my years in Riverside, I have been involved in many community organizations: NAACP, Urban League, and North High School Site Council to name a few. But one individual that I especially came to admire was Willie Brown. I heard Mr. Brown speak (at least twice) at NAACP functions in Riverside, and I was impressed with his presentations. Mr. Brown went on to become speaker of the California State Assembly followed by two terms as mayor of San Francisco. In his presentations to the NAACP, Willie said that it was his goal to become so well known that when introduced, there would be no need for long, drawn-out introductions. He said he wanted to become so well known that the person introducing him would only have to say, "Ladies and gentlemen, Mr. Willie Brown," like they introduce the president of the United States. I think he darn near achieved that status as speaker of the California State Assembly. Mr. Brown was very effective in getting his bills approved; he was so effective that term-limits were approved that removed him from office.

You should not strive to simply be good at what you do but try to be the best at it. That is what Willie Brown did, and it's an example we should follow. But try not to let your ambition be selfish. Try to make whatever you are involved in better than how you found it. Do this for everyone's benefit. If you work hard and unselfishly, you will receive the recognition you deserve and sometimes recognition that you don't deserve.

Election Night: November4, 2008

I would like to share with you my feelings on that history making night November 4, 2008 when Barrack Obama was elected President of the United States of America:Tonight I watched anxiously, with great concern and high expectations, as the early returns began to trickle in. That morning I had delayed my walk because of an early morning rain. When I did take my walk at about eight o'clock, my route took me through a residential area that had been one of my routes as a mail carrier back in the early 1970s. There were lots of campaign signs for "McCain-Palin" in the residents' yards, which for some reason made me remember a kid calling me a name while I was delivering mail. I recall the mother rushing out and reprimanding the kid. My response to the mother was, "He's only repeating what he's heard from others," and continued delivering the mail. But I was deeply hurt . . .

Here I sit tonight waiting for a Black man—Barrack Obama—to be elected president of the United States of America. If successful, he will be the first Black president in the history of our nation. Suddenly Senator Obama moves ahead in electoral votes in the early returns; he wins Ohio, Pennsylvania, and he is running strong in Virginia and Florida. I am watching CNN, and at eight o'clock, he is declared the winner! I never thought I would see a Black president in my lifetime, but I recalled the words in Dr. King's sermon the night before he was murdered. He said, "I have been to the mountaintop, I have looked over and have seen the promised land; I may not get there with you, but you will get to the promised land."

Metrolink: Perris Line

When I was appointed to the board of the Riverside County Transportation Commission (RCTC), there were discussions concerning a rail line for Metrolink from Perris to Riverside. The discussions were about the loop's location. Would the line go all the way into Highgrove and loop back down into Riverside, or would the loop take place earlier, perhaps near Columbia Street? Citizens of Highgrove often addressed the board and requested their own station.

Other discussions ensued about the location of stations along the line from Perris into Riverside. Ought there to be a station near March Air Reserve Base? Should there be one in the University (UCR) area near Watkins and Blaine Street? We solicited input from the citizens in the UCR area. We wanted their suggestions and concerns. Over the years, we held many such meetings, both while I was a board member and afterward. As a councilman and a board member, I had dual concerns: as a councilman, I represented the area; as a board member, I wanted to do what was best for Metrolink riders and protect the interests of the people in the area. After numerous meeting in the area, the problems and concerns seemed to be resolved, and RCTC prepared for construction. However, just last week (August 26, 2011) there was an article in the *Press Enterprise* stating opposition concerning the line from a group known as Friends of Riverside Hills. The leaders of this group live in the area and had more than ample time to voice their concerns. I hope their effort does not delay this project, because it will not only provide a needed service for commuters but also provide jobs that will help to boost the economy and reduce congestion on the freeway.

Sometimes, we need to weigh immediate concerns against future needs. One thing in this world that is constant is change; let us try to anticipate what those changes are going to be and plan to address them. Where there is no vision the people perish.

Fireworks at UCR-Riverside Stadium

There is nothing like watching a fireworks display on the Fourth of July. They make me think about the history of our nation, its ideals of freedom and equality. The preamble to the Constitution says, "We the People of the United States, in Order to form a more perfect Union, establish Justice, insure domestic Tranquility, provide for the common defense, promote the general Welfare and secure the Blessings of Liberty to ourselves and our Posterity, do ordain and establish this Constitution for the United States of America."

We have come a long way since the days of slavery—we currently have a Black president. We still have a ways to go as a race before we can consider ourselves to be on an equal footing in this nation, but I would not want to live anyplace else. The ideals, values, the freedoms rooted in this country keep our hope alive.

As a councilman, I was successful in bringing fireworks on the Fourth of July to the UCR-Riverside Stadium. We were able to do so for very little cost to the City of Riverside. Everyone paid a small stipend to view the fireworks except for children five years old and under. The stadium was usually packed for this event, so the fireworks essentially paid for themselves.

Actually, I was baffled when I discovered that the fireworks display had been discontinued after I left the council. I must say I was very disappointed. I just cannot understand why you would discontinue a patriotic, well-attended event that was paying its own way. Several other areas in the city had fireworks on the Fourth of July, but none that paid their own cost. Oh well; it was fun while it lasted. I looked forward to it every year when I was on the council and attended with friends and relatives. They were appreciative and very impressed. We always left the stadium proud to be Americans.

Pilots

Another tradition that came and left the UCR-Riverside Stadium was the Pilots—a Minor League Baseball club that brought pride and prestige to the community. I know firsthand that they would have liked to stay in Riverside, but their revenue was greatly diminished because they were not allowed to sell beer at the stadium.

Now what baseball club do you know—Major or Minor League—that does not sell beer? I have been to two Minor League clubs in the area—Lake Elsinore and San Bernardino—and both cities allow their Minor League team to sell beer, and, as far as I am aware, no significant incidents have occurred due to the sale of beer. Citizens in Riverside did not want the stadium to sell beer because they believed it would promote drunk driving in the area. In my estimation, college students are mostly responsible for drunk driving in the area, and beer sales at the stadium would not greatly increase the problem.

I am not a drinker, so the sale of beer or the lack thereof has no effect on me. But a very significant amount of revenue is lost to a Minor League ball club when they are not allowed to sell beer; if they had been allowed to sell beer, the team would probably still be in Riverside sharing revenue and providing entertainment to people of all ages.

Ancestry

You never know how meaningful it is to know your grandparents: what they looked like; from whom they descended; what their childhood was like; what their dreams(s) were growing up, and whether they accomplished them, etc. These are some of the questions I would have asked my grandparents if I had had the privilege of meeting them.

Mom talked about her dad frequently to us children, but we never saw a picture of him; sure, we had the mental picture Mom painted of him but not a physical picture. There was nothing I could point to and say, "That's my granddad on Mom's side of the family." In December, 2010, I was blessed to obtain a picture of my mom's mother, my grandmother; she was a beautiful light-skinned lady. Her name was Mary Etta Webb. Boy, how I would have enjoyed talking with her. I would love to have heard firsthand her thoughts; her dreams; her likes and dislikes; and who her ancestors were. But I thank God I at least now have a picture of her and know what she looked like.

Dad told us who his parents were: His father was Joseph (Joe) Moore and his mother's name was Clarab (I don't know what her last name was before marriage). In any event, I never saw them and do not have their pictures, so I don't know what they looked like. You do not realize how meaningful pictures are until you are without them. They are a treasure—memories frozen in time.

I regret I do not have a picture of my brother Oneal dressed in his sheriff uniform, of which he was so proud. I think his grandchildren and their children would be very proud to have a picture of a very courageous relative that opened doors of opportunity for his people. He lost his life in the process and never received justice, but I am so very proud of his contribution to the civil rights movement.

There is nothing wrong with asking people questions—you gain knowledge and history that will be lost to the future. It's good to have a curious mind. Curious-minded individuals are very bright. They want to know: why, who, and how. In obtaining answers to these questions, they acquire a lot of knowledge. As a father and a grandfather, I enjoy passing on my heritage to my family. So, ask your relatives questions in order to learn more about who you are and who your ancestors were. You may be pleasantly surprised, motivated, and inspired.

Summary

Someone has said that the greatest barrier to achievement is fear of failure. Many times we have brilliant ideas but do not act upon them because we fear we will fail. I wonder how many times the Wright brothers failed before they finally soared. When I visit Washington, DC, I like to tour the Space Museum. At the entrance to the Museum hangs a small biplane—I assume this plane was our first venture off the ground. The Wright brothers had the idea that if birds can fly, why can't I? In other words, as someone has said, "If you can conceive it, you can achieve it." However, you may fail many times before you succeed. The important thing is to learn from your mistakes and keep at it.

Sometimes I wonder if we challenge ourselves enough. Do we stretch ourselves? Do we strive to reach our full potential in life? Don't get comfortable where you are—put all your energy into reaching your full potential. We cheat ourselves when we do not give our best effort.

Pursue your dream in life. If you don't have a dream, come up with one. Make it something that excites you; something that puts fire in your belly; something that gives meaning to your life; something that you know you have the talent to do. You only go around once in life, so put God first and pursue your dream. Don't go to your grave with the music still in you.

Having a dream gives you a reason for getting out of bed other than just going to a job you don't like, but need, in order to put bread on the table for yourself and your family.

Try to surround yourself with achievers and dreamers—people that will inspire and encourage you, people that are always looking for ways to improve themselves. Regardless of how good we are, we can be better. We should never stop learning. The more you know, the more you realize you don't know. Learning can be exciting at any age, but it is especially exciting when you are young. Your imagination is keener, your energy level is higher, and the odds are that you have a lot of years left to achieve your dreams and put them into action.

Avoid blaming others for your shortcomings or failures because, ultimately, you are responsible for you. Accept responsibility for your actions—good or bad. Let your successes motivate you, and learn from your mistakes. Remember the definition of an idiot: "Someone who does the same thing over and over and expects a different result."

Value and appreciate your friends because true friends are hard to find. Also, know your enemies.

Learn to listen; neither you nor anyone else has a monopoly on knowledge. You can learn from the uneducated as well as the educated. Respect people for who they are—individuals created in God's image. Separate the good from the bad, but remember there is some good in the worst of us and some bad in the best of us. If you don't listen, you might miss out on some valuable information that might help you achieve your dreams.

Learn to enjoy the simple things in life: a beautiful sunset, a lovely sunrise (new day), and a diverse cloud formation. These things cost you nothing but are evident of the Almighty's hand at work. I remember seeing the most beautiful sunset in Jamaica in 1984, when Henrietta and I spent a week's vacation there. It was a clear day, and the sun appeared to go down into the ocean, its rays a gorgeous red; it was awe-inspiring to me.

A sunrise brings in a new day—a day not promised to you but one your creator blessed you to see and enjoy. Make the best of it: fill it with kindness to yourself and to others you may encounter during the day. You just might brighten someone's day with a lovely smile and a warm, sincere greeting. Being kind to others also makes you feel better about yourself.

I grew up in the country, and I can remember spending hours lying under a shade tree looking up into the sky and watching the clouds take on different shapes. I would imagine seeing the faces of animals, humans, states, continents, etc. You name it, and I have imagined seeing it among the clouds in the sky. I believe you have to imagine yourself where you want to be before you can achieve it.

Finally, listen to that still, soft voice that speaks to you and follow its lead; it will lead you to success and fulfillment.

About the Author

I was born in Camp Rowling, a logging town in southern Mississippi. A logging camp moved about from place to place following the timber. My dad, Stephen Moore, supervised the making of crossties for the railroad for Mr. Lewis.

My dad bought a four-room bungalow house in 1938, and we became permanent residents on a ten-acre plot of land in White Sand, Mississippi, a rural area about five miles west of Poplarville, Mississippi. I enlisted in the U.S. Air Force in December 1954, took basic training at Lackland Air Force Base, Texas; teletype communication training at Chyenne, Wyoming; cryptographic training at Scott Field, Illinois; spent eighteen months at Clark Air Force Base in the Philippines. I returned to the states in 1957, and married my high school sweetheart, Henrietta; stationed briefly at Lockport Air Station up state New York; worked two years at the National Security Agency, Ft. Meade, Maryland. Following my second four year enlistment in 1958, and a year's our at Thule Greenland, I was reassigned to March Air Force Base, Riverside, California in 1960 and have lived here ever since.